MY WEE GRANNY'S FU

Traditional Scottish Recip

From

My Wee Granny's Table to Yours

Angela Hossack

Dedicated to my wee granny –
Annie Clark
1890-1971

MY WEE GRANNY'S FULL TABLE

Also by Angela Hossack

MY WEE GRANNY'S OLD Scottish Recipes

My Wee Granny's Bannocks and Bakes

My Wee Granny's Soups and Stews

Copyright Angela Hossack 2019

The right of Angela Hossack to be identified as author of this work has been asserted in accordance with the Copyright, Designs and Patents Act 1988.

ISBN: 9781092579568

Imprint: Independently published

CONTENTS

- Introduction
- Tasty wee bites to start your meal

– canapes, hors d'oeuvres and savory starters done the Scottish way

- Catsups, Stuffings and Sauces
- Stock
- Soups
- Fish Dishes
- Side Dishes
- Poultry
- Game and other Meat Dishes
- Stews
- Bridies and Pies
- Bannocks
- Scones
- Sweet Puddings and Pies
- Cakes and Sweet Loaves
- Biscuits and Shortbread

INTRODUCTION

MY FAMILY HAVE CHOPPED, sliced, braised, fried, roasted, baked and ate these dishes across five generations. Some of these recipes were written in little notebooks, on the back of cook books, on scraps of paper, and some have been simply handed down through word of mouth from my wee granny, to my granny, to my mammie, to me and my sisters, and to daughters and nieces.

They are traditional and authentic Scottish recipes and utterly delicious. They are simple to follow – using simple ingredients and simple cooking and baking methods – and you won't fail to experience a true taste of Scotland.

This book incorporates every single recipe and they are served from My Wee Granny's table to yours.

Enjoy.

WEE TASTY BITES AND STARTERS

Sautéed Sweetbreads and Asparagus

WHAT YOU WILL NEED:

200g of lamb's sweetbreads

600g of asparagus

2 tablespoons of butter

Salt and pepper

What you need to do:

Add the sweetbreads to a pan of boiling water and simmer for a few minutes, then drain and allow to cool. Remove the membranes.

Cook the asparagus in boiling water for approximately five minutes

When cold, slice the sweetbreads – being careful to make clean slices.

Melt the butter in a large frying pan and gently sauté the sliced sweetbreads, Remove and then toss the asparagus in the butter.

Spicy Cauliflower Fritters

MAKES 12 FRITTERS

<u>What you will need:</u>

1 small cauliflower cut into florets

60g of plain flour

1 shallot

1 clove of garlic

Half a teaspoon of turmeric

1 red chili

Salt and pepper

2 eggs

Vegetable oil (for your deep-fat fryer)

<u>What you need to do:</u>

Finely dice the shallot and mince the garlic

De-seed and finely chop the chili

Put the flour, turmeric, chili, garlic and shallot into a bowl and mix thoroughly. Season with salt and pepper, beat the eggs and add to the mix – ensuring the mixture is well combined. Put to the side

Add the cauliflower florets to slightly salted boiling water and simmer for approximately 3 or 4 minutes, drain and plunge into iced water. When cool, drain and add to the bowl with the other ingredients and gently mix.

Use a tablespoon to place the mixture carefully into the pre-heated vegetable oil (you should get approximately 12 separate fritters from the mix) and fry until golden.

Goat's Cheese and Red Pepper Tartlet

WHAT YOU WILL NEED:

4 red bell peppers

2 tablespoons of olive oil

180g of goat's cheese

2 tablespoons of cream

1 egg yolk

Cold water (enough to combine the pastry)

50g of butter

100g of plain flour

Baking beans and greaseproof paper

What you need to do:

Rub the olive oil onto the peppers and roast in a hot oven for 15 minutes. Remove the seeds and roughly chop.

Make the pastry by rubbing the butter into the flour to make a breadcrumb consistency, then add the water to combine. Chill in the fridge in clingfilm for 30 minutes. Once chilled, split the dough into 4 equal parts, roll out and line 4 4-inch tart tins. Put greaseproof paper on top of the pastry and add the baking beans. Bake in a hot oven (200 degrees C) for 10 minutes. Remove the beans and paper and return to the oven for a further 5 minutes. Allow to cool.

Mix the goat's cheese with the cream and the egg yolk and season with salt and pepper.

Divide the peppers amongst the 4 pastry cases. Spoon the goat's cheese on top and return to the oven for approximately 8 minutes.

Roasted Vegetable and Cheddar Cheese Tartlet

WHAT YOU WILL NEED:

2 red onions

2 yellow bell peppers

2 red bell peppers

1 clove of garlic

4 button mushrooms

2 tablespoons of olive oil

200g of grated cheddar cheese

What you need to do:

Roughly chop the onions

Quarter the peppers and remove the seeds

Finely chop/dice the mushrooms

Finely chop the garlic

Mix everything through the olive oil and place in a roasting tin. Put in a hot oven for 15 minutes

Follow the previous recipe to make the pastry tarts

Divide the roasted vegetables amongst 4 pastry shells and top with the grated cheese. Return to the oven for approximately 5 minutes.

Seared Scallops with Black Pudding and Haggis Crumb

WHAT YOU WILL NEED:

12 scallops

2 black pudding rounds

2 slices of haggis

1 tablespoon of butter

1 tablespoon of vegetable oil

Salt and pepper

What you need to do:

Ensure that the scallops are room temperature

Fry the black pudding and the haggis in the vegetable oil

In a separate, large, HOT frying pan, gently fry the scallops in the butter (approximately 1minute each side) until they are golden. If they are large scallops, they may need an extra 30 seconds or so on each side

Crumble the haggis and the black pudding and divide into 4. Each serving is 3 scallops. Season to taste.

Seared Scallops with Quail's Egg

WHAT YOU WILL NEED:

12 scallops

4 quail's eggs

2 tablespoon of butter

Salt and pepper

What you need to do:

Fry the scallops (see previous recipe) in 1 tablespoon of butter

In another small, non-stick, frying pan, fry the quail's eggs leaving the yolks runny

Serve 3 scallops with a quail's egg on top per portion

Season with salt and pepper to taste

Roasted Pork Belly Bites with Baked Apple

WHAT YOU WILL NEED:

800g of boned pork belly (skin on)

4 apples

1 tablespoon of butter

Salt

What you need to do:

Thoroughly dry the pork belly, season with salt and place in a moderate oven (170 degrees C). Roast for 2 and a half hours and ensure the skin is golden and crackly

Meantime, core the apples and rub with the butter then place in an ovenproof dish, cover with foil and bake for approximately 45 minutes to 1 hour

When the pork is cooked and rested, cut into cubes and serve with the baked apple

Lobster and Fennel Salad

WHAT YOU WILL NEED:

1 lobster (live)

4 baby fennel bulbs

1 clove of garlic

100mls of white wine

2 tablespoons of butter

4 spring onions

1 teaspoon of black peppercorns

salt

What you need to do:

Bring a large pot of water to the boil and add the wine, garlic, peppercorns and whole lobster. Boil for 8 minutes

Meantime, halve the fennel bulbs and fry in the butter until soft

Remove the lobster and, when cool, remove the meat – leaving it as intact as possible, then slice and divide into 4 portions

Finely dice the spring onions

Serve the lobster on top of the fennel and garnish with the spring onions

Bite-sized Potato Cakes with Monkfish and Bacon

WHAT YOU WILL NEED:

4 monkfish fillets

6 slices of streaky bacon (smoked)

400g of potatoes

1 egg

40g of plain flour

2 tablespoons of butter

1 tablespoon of vegetable oil

50g of fresh breadcrumbs

Salt and pepper

What you need to do:

Peel and boil the potatoes in salted water, then drain and mash with one tablespoon of the butter. Allow to thoroughly cool.

Meantime, slice each of the monkfish fillets into 3 portions and cut the bacon into 12 pieces. Wrap each piece of monkfish in a portion of the bacon and fry in the vegetable oil for a minute or so, then finish off in a hot oven for approximately 5 minutes.

Beat the egg. Shape the potato mixture into 12 portions, dip in the egg, flatten into cakes and coat in the breadcrumbs.

Fry the potato cakes for a minute each side in the remaining butter

Serve a piece of the monkfish on top of the cakes.

Smoked Mackerel Pate

PREPARE IN ADVANCE

What you will need:

4 smoked mackerel fillets

4 tablespoons of creamed cheese

Quarter of a red onion

1 teaspoon of lemon juice

1 teaspoon of butter

1 teaspoon of fine brandy

Salt and pepper

What you need to do:

Finely mince the red onion

Thoroughly mix and combine the cream cheese, butter, onion, lemon juice and brandy. Season with salt and pepper.

Flake the smoked mackerel through the mix and spoon into 4 ramekins. Cover with cling-film and put in the fridge for at least 4 hours.

Crab cakes

WHAT YOU WILL NEED:

600g of cooked, flaked crab meat

400g of potatoes

2 egg

40g of plain flour

2 tablespoons of butter

100g of fresh breadcrumbs

Salt and pepper

1 teaspoon of lemon juice

What you need to do:

Peel and boil the potatoes in salted water, then drain and mash with one tablespoon of the butter. Allow to thoroughly cool, then mix through the flaked crab meat and the lemon juice. Season to taste with the salt and pepper

Beat the eggs. Shape the potato mixture into 8 portions, dip in the egg, flatten into cakes and coat in the breadcrumbs.

Fry the potato cakes in the remaining butter until golden brown on both sides

Tiger Prawns with Creamy Whisky Sauce

WHAT YOU WILL NEED:

12 tiger prawns, de-shelled and de-veined

500ml of double cream

2 teaspoons of wholegrain mustard

1 tablespoon of Dijon mustard

2 teaspoons of whisky

sea salt and freshly ground white pepper

1 tablespoon of chopped fresh chives

1 tablespoon of lemon juice

1 tablespoon of butter

Salt and pepper

What you need to do:

Add the cream to a saucepan and heat through gently then add the 2 mustards and the whisky. Stir and increase the heat to a simmer. Simmer for a couple of minutes then remove from the heat. Add the chopped chives and the lemon juice and season with the salt and pepper.

Meantime, butterfly the tiger prawns and fry gently in the butter until cooked – being careful not to overcook.

Serve 3 per portion topped with the whisky sauce.

Guinea Fowl with Beetroot Relish

WHAT YOU WILL NEED:

4 guinea fowl breasts

8 baby beetroot

2 shallots

1 teaspoon of sugar

1 teaspoon of lime juice

1 teaspoon of finely chopped flat leafed parsley

1 teaspoon of malt vinegar

1 tablespoon of butter

Salt and pepper

What you will need to do:

Scrub and wrap the beetroot in foil and bake in a moderate to hot oven for 45 minutes. When cooked, peel and dice and put in a bowl.

Finely dice the shallots and add to the bowl along with the parsley, sugar, lime juice and vinegar. Mix thoroughly.

Fry the guinea fowl breasts in the butter ensuring it is served pink

CATSUPS, STUFFINGS AND SAUCES

MY WEE GRANNY'S FULL TABLE

Walnut Catsup

YOU NEED TO MAKE IT in advance and keep in an airtight jar.

Ensure that your walnuts are not too hard.

To prepare before cooking - take 50 walnuts and squeeze them a little to bruise them and put in a jar with 1 tablespoon of salt and half a litre of vinegar. You then need to allow to marinade for at least a week.

Once marinated, put them in a pot with a teaspoon of nutmeg, a teaspoon of cloves, a teaspoon of ginger a teaspoon of black peppercorns a cm of horseradish 10 small shallots, 200g of anchovies and 250mls (half a pint) of port.

Boil and simmer for half an hour. Taste and add more vinegar or wine if required.

You can either strain and then use the liquid or use the catsup without straining. Store in an airtight jar or bottle.

Mussel Catsup

BOIL 900G OF MUSSELS in two and a half cups of sherry. When the mussels are cooked, remove from their shells, mash with a potato masher and return to the cooking liquor. Add 2 teaspoons of salt and a quarter of a teaspoon of cayenne pepper and 4 anchovies. Bring back to the boil and skim.

Strain and store in airtight jars

Liquid Mushroom Catsup

900G (2LBS) OF CHESTNUT mushrooms, 2 teaspoons of salt, 2 bay leaves, 1 chopped onion, the zest of 1 lemon, a quarter of a teaspoon of Allspice, a quarter of a teaspoon of cayenne pepper, I tablespoon of horseradish that has been finely grated, a quarter of a teaspoon of cloves and half a cup of cider vinegar.

Carefully wipe and chop the mushrooms then put in a bowl with the salt and the bay leaves, mash them slightly with a potato masher, pat the mixture flat, cover and leave overnight to draw out the liquid.

The next day, add the chopped onion, the lemon zest, the horseradish, the Allspice, the cloves and the cayenne pepper. Stir in the cider vinegar.

Bring to the boil and simmer for 20 minutes.

Strain all the juice and put the liquid mushroom catsup it in an airtight jar or bottle.

Oyster Catsup

KEEP THE OYSTER LIQUOR and pound 16 shucked and cleaned oysters, then add the liquor and two and a half cups of sherry.

Bring to the boil, then add 2 teaspoons of salt and a quarter of a teaspoon of cayenne pepper.

Take off the boil and skim.

Strain and return to the pot and stir in a tablespoon of brandy.

Store in airtight jars.

Cucumber Catsup

SLICE 6 CUCUMBERS AND mix with 4 chopped onions. Add 2 teaspoons of salt, cover and leave to sit for 36 hours. Strain and add a teaspoon of chopped horseradish, the peel of 1 lemon, black pepper and a quarter of a teaspoon of cayenne pepper. Bring to the boil and simmer for 15 minutes. Strain once more and add 2 teaspoons of brandy.

Store in airtight bottles.

Basic Breadcrumb Stuffing

THIS BASIC BREADCRUMB stuffing forms the basis of most stuffing.

Mix 1 cup of breadcrumbs with half a cup of finely chopped flat leaf parsley. Season with salt and pepper, add a knob of butter, a teaspoon of grated lemon peel, a tablespoon of suet, a teaspoon of thyme and a quarter of a grated nutmeg. Beat 2 egg yolks and mix through thoroughly.

Liver Stuffing

Add the (chopped) liver of your choice (rabbit, chicken, wildfowl, lamb) to the basic breadcrumb stuffing. Chop one boiled egg and one rasher of chopped bacon and add to the mix.

Mushroom and Pine Nut Stuffing

To the basic breadcrumb stuffing mix, add 1 chopped onion, 4 cloves of finely sliced garlic, 500g of chopped chestnut mushrooms, 1 beaten egg and a half a cup of pine nuts.

Oyster and Ham Stuffing

TO THE BASIC BREADCRUMB mix add one cup of chopped pickled oysters and one cup of chopped ham.

SAGE AND ONION STUFFING

To the basic breadcrumb stuffing mix add 3 teaspoons of dried sage.

HAGGIS STUFFING

This stuffing does not use the basic breadcrumb stuffing mix.

Either use 200g of premade haggis or make from scratch.

To make from scratch –cook 1 cup of oats, and mix in chopped lambs lungs, lambs liver, lambs heart and half a cup of shredded beef suet. Chop 2 onions and add. Season with salt and pepper. And mix thoroughly.

Sweet Stuffing

1 CUP OF BREADCRUMBS, 250mls of chicken stock, 200g of butter, one and a half cups of chopped celery (remove fibrous stringy bits), 1 chopped onion, 3 chopped large sweet apples, 225 g of chopped water chestnuts (one 8oz can), 1 tablespoon sugar, half a teaspoon of black pepper.

Make applesauce from one of the apples. Bring the stock to the boil and mix all of the ingredients, put in an ovenproof dish and bake in a medium pre-heated oven until browned.

Caper Sauce

1 TABLESPOON OF CAPERS (crushed), 2 tablespoons of butter, juice of 1 lemon, salt and pepper.

Melt half of the butter in a small frying pan, add the crushed capers and sauté for a few seconds and then add the lemon juice and the salt and pepper. Continue to sauté on a low heat for a couple of minutes and then remove from the head.

Add the remaining butter and mix thoroughly.

Brown Sauce

2 TART APPLES (PEELED, cored and chopped), half a cup of pitted prunes (chopped), 2 brown onions (diced), half a cup of malt vinegar, 2 tablespoons of sugar, teaspoon of salt, tablespoon of Worcester sauce, a clove of garlic, half a teaspoon of ground ginger and half a teaspoon of allspice.

Simply put everything into a blender and mix thoroughly.

Put the mixture into a tightly sealed saucepan and simmer gently for 3 hours.

Sauce for Wildfowl (version one)

BRING 200MLS OF CHICKEN stock to the boil and add a quarter of a cup of breadcrumbs, 3 chopped shallots, a half a glass of claret, salt and pepper. Simmer for 15 minutes.

Sauce for Wildfowl (version two)

A SLICE OF BREAD BOILED in a little chicken stock, a chopped onion, 2 cloves, a knob of butter, half a glass of white wine and a tablespoon of mushroom catsup, simmered together in a pan for 15 minutes.

Sauce for Venison version one

A SIMPLE SAUCE MADE from 2 glasses of claret that has been boiled and simmered until it reduces and becomes very thick. Add to this a tablespoon of redcurrant or blackcurrant jelly.

Sauce for Venison version two

This is a sharp sauce.

200g of sugar that has been dissolved in 250mls of champagne vinegar. Skim.

Liver Sauce for Poultry

A CUP OF CHICKEN STOCK, half a cup of finely chopped chicken livers, 1 chopped onion, half a cup of chopped celery (with fibrous stringy bits removed), a heaped teaspoon of corn flour.

Gently fry the livers, the onion and the celery in a teaspoon of vegetable oil.

Use a little of the cold stock to mix the corn flour. Bring remaining stock to the boil and add the other ingredients. Simmer for 15 minutes and thicken with the cornflour.

Liver Sauce for Game

FOLLOW THE RECIPE FOR liver sauce for poultry but replace the stock with rich beef stock and replace the livers with venison livers. Add a chopped and gently fried rasher of bacon.

Drappit Egg Sauce

Bring 1 cup of chicken stock to the boil and fork in 2 beaten eggs. Mix in 2 tablespoons of chopped flat leaf parsley.

Oyster sauce

Shuck 250 g of oysters. Keep the liquor. Very finely chop the oysters and add to the liquid. Bring to the boil, cover and simmer for 10 minutes. Remove from the heat and add a teaspoon of salt. Once cooled, sieve and add 2 tablespoons of soy sauce.

Celery sauce

REMOVE THE FIBROUS stringy bits from a whole celery, chop and add to a pan with boiling water for five minutes. Add a quarter of an inch of grated nutmeg, and season with salt and pepper. Meanwhile, put 2 tablespoons of butter and 2 tablespoons of flour in a pan, stir over a low heat until browned then add to the pan with the celery. Mix thoroughly.

Creamy Cider and Mustard Sauce

300MLS OF CIDER, 1 TABLESPOON of wholegrain mustard, 300mls of double cream, black pepper

Boil the cider until it reduces by about half of its volume, then add the cream and mix thoroughly. Simmer until the sauce thickens. Add the mustard, mix, and season with black pepper.

Mustard Sauce

200MLS OF VEGETABLE STOCK, 1 onion (diced), 1 carrot (diced), 1 stalk of celery (take out the stringy bits and chop), 2 teaspoons of mustard (of your choice), 1 tablespoon of honey, 1 teaspoon of butter.

Sauté the vegetables in the butter until soft and then gently mash with a fork. Add to the stock and simmer, with lid off, until the stock reduces by a third. Strain through a fine colander and then add and mix through the mustard and the honey.

Tomato Sauce

---

4 TOMATOES (BLANCHED, peeled, deseeded and chopped), 2 shallots (chopped), 1 clove of garlic (finely minced), 1 teaspoon of lemon juice, 1 tablespoon of extra virgin olive oil.

Put everything in a pan, mix thoroughly and simmer on a low heat for 5 minutes.

STOCK FOR SOUPS, STEWS, GRAVIES AND SAUCES

IT'S ALL ABOUT THE STOCK

FIRST, A WORD OR TWO about seasoning your stock.

Those of you, who are as old as I am, may remember when everything we ate seemed to be so much tastier than the food we eat now. One of the reasons could be that more salt and more fat was used. Back in the day, there wasn't the health warnings that we're all now used to hearing about reducing our salt and fat intake. We didn't know about cholesterol and high blood pressure and the effects of salt and fat on those conditions, but we know now and, so, we have to look to healthier means of seasoning our stocks.

A little salt and a little fat will continue to be used in my wee granny's stock recipes, but other ingredients – some of which she used and some of which I added to replace the lost salt and fat – have found their way into my stockpots over the years. I've experimented with these ingredients and find that they don't take away from the basic deliciousness of my wee granny's soups and stews.

It goes without saying that you can't make a good pot of soup or stew, gravy, or sauce without a rich base stock. Traditionally, stockpots were on the go all of the time – simmering away over the fire or on the stove with bones and leftovers continuously replenishing it. These days, some home cooks tend to use stock cubes, but I find that relying on cubes alone leads to a soup or stew with very little body.

My wee granny always had her base stocks prepared in advance. I follow in her footsteps and tend to either make my stock the day before I need it or make a huge pot and freeze it.

The most important thing to remember about a good stock is that it needs time… hours and hours of time, but you don't have to stand over it and watch it. You can leave it alone. Just throw your bits and pieces in the pot, cover with water, put a tight lid on and leave it alone for at least four hours, but preferably longer.

Something else that's very important – throw nothing away. Keep and freeze every chicken, turkey and duck carcass. Keep and freeze every trimming from every meat you've used to cook with. Save the lamb bone from the leg you have on Sunday. Oven roast and then keep beef bones, ox tail bones and pork bones. Waste nothing… including skin and fat. If you haven't used the juices from a roast for gravy – don't discard – keep for your stockpot. And, what about the outside celery stalks that you tend to discard, or the stalks of broccoli and cauliflower? The outside leaves and stalks of cabbages? The leftover raw or cooked vegetables? Yes, you've guessed it – throw in the stockpot. Just make sure everything is washed under cold running water first.

Your basic **vegetable stock** – scrubbed and chopped carrots with their skins left on, the outside celery stalks that you tend to discard, a couple of whole onions, the outside leaves and the end root of the leek (or a whole leek if you have one going spare), cabbage, broccoli and cauliflower stalks, leftover raw and cooked vegetables and a whole garlic bulb (roasted whole first). Use also any leftover salad tomatoes, spring onions (scallions), sweetcorn, peas and peppers. Put everything in a pot with water (The amount of water will depend on how much bits and pieces you've added to the pot, but you must at least ensure everything is covered by water and then add a further 2 cups), put it on to boil, cover with a tight lid, simmer and forget about it.

When it has simmered for at least four hours, carefully drain through a fine colander, ensuring you squeeze out every last bit of stock and then discard the veggie bits and pieces.

Leave the seasoning until after you have drained and sieved through the colander and, this way, you won't lose any of the seasoning with the discarded vegetables. Season to taste with a little salt, white pepper, celery salt, onion salt and (if preferred, a little garlic paste).

I use **chicken stock** a lot. We eat a lot of chicken in our house and my freezer is usually crammed with carcasses. I have a stock pot that can take up to 8 carcasses.

For added flavour I roast the carcasses in the oven for 30 minutes before throwing them in the stockpot, covering with water, bringing to the boil and simmering under a tight lid for at least 6 hours. I give it a stir now and again and top up with water if necessary, otherwise I leave it alone and get on with other things. Straining can be a bit of a pain, but it's worth it.

Season to taste with salt, white pepper, celery salt and onion salt. I also add a little ground turmeric to my chicken stock.

If possible, make your chicken stock the day before you need it because it is always best refrigerated, and most of the fat then skimmed off the top. It will amaze you just how much fat will float and set on the surface and its then up to you how much of that fat you allow to remain in your stock.

You only actually get about 4 pints of stock from 8 carcasses, but you can imagine how rich and delicious it is.

You can, of course, make smaller amounts of chicken stock. If I know that I want stock for a gravy, or a curry or a small pot of soup or stew the day after I roast a chicken, then I immediately get the carcass on to simmer. A single carcass is simmered for about 3 hours and I get just under a pint of stock.

At Christmas, or other holiday periods, you may have turkey, duck, geese carcasses etc and you can add them to the stockpot with your chicken carcasses to make a **mixed fowl stock** or – in the case of turkey – make a standalone **turkey stock**.

Mixed meat stock – made with any or all of your yummy lamb, beef, ox tail and that you have to hand, as well as any meat trimmings or any leftover cooked or uncooked meats. Always roast the bones and trimmings for 30 minutes before adding to your stockpot. Roasting begins the caramelising process and adds a tremendous amount of flavour. Cover with water and bring to the boil. Remove all the scum that forms on the top (this will ensure a nice clear stock).

Gently simmer for as long as you can, but for at least 4 hours. Strain carefully ensuring you get every drop of stock and leave to cool then put in the fridge overnight so that the fat solidifies on top and then skim.

Season to taste with salt, pepper, celery salt and onion salt. I also add a little ground chilli (quarter of a teaspoon) to my mixed meat stock, but this is optional.

Rich beef stock is a bit more expensive to make because it doesn't just rely on bones and trimmings. Hough (shin) and brisket are the staples for a good, rich beef stock along with any beef bones and trimmings, but the meat can then be used for a variety of dishes.

Seal the shin and brisket in a frying pan and add to your stockpot. Roast any beef bones or beef trimmings to hand and then add. Cover with water and bring it to a gentle simmer. After it has simmered for at least 3 hours, remove the shin and the joint of brisket and then continue simmering the bones and trimmings for at least another hour – preferably longer. Season to taste with salt, lots of black pepper, onion salt and celery salt.

Your rich beef stock can be enhanced with the addition of ox tails or you can make a pure **Ox tail stock.** Ox tails are delicious, and you can use the meaty bones afterwards. Make your ox tail stock as you would a mixed meat or beef stock, remembering to skim off the scum when it comes to the boil. Season to taste.

A favourite stock of my wee granny was a simple **vegetable, and breast/neck of lamb stock.**

This stock forms the basis of many soups and stews. To the ingredients of the basic vegetable stock, add a roasted breast of lamb and roasted lamb neck bones and follow the method for making the rich beef stock, removing the breast of lamb after 3 hours. Continue to simmer the vegetable and neck bones for a further hour then carefully drain and sieve.

Season to taste with salt, pepper, celery salt and onion salt. Garlic paste and a quarter of a teaspoon of chilli powder can be added, but these are optional.

For **Smoked or unsmoked ham stock** you need celery stalks, a large leek, a large onion, a couple of carrots and a smoked or unsmoked gammon or ham hock and/or cuts of smoked or unsmoked bacon. Cover with water and bring to a slow boil. Remove the scum formed on the top and simmer for 3 hours. Drain carefully and season to taste with salt, white pepper, celery salt and onion salt. Cool and leave in fridge overnight and skim and discard the fat that has congealed on the top.

Basic fish stock – fish heads and bones fried for a few minutes gently in butter alongside a roughly chopped onion, 2 stalks of roughly chopped celery and roughly chopped stalks of parsley. Season with celery salt, thyme, a bay leaf, salt and pepper then put in your stock pot, add a cup of white wine to every litre of water and simmer for one hour. Strain through a sieve. For a **richer shellfish stock** use the heads and shells of prawns, lobster shells, razor fish shells and the strained liquor of mussels and follow the method for your basic fish stock but cook out for an additional 30 minutes.

SOUPS

VEGETABLE SOUPS

Kale and Oatmeal Soup

SERVES 4

What you will need:

1 litre of vegetable stock

4 cups (chopped) Green kale (240g)

Quarter of a cup of oatmeal (32g)

Half a cup (150ml) double cream

What you need to do:

Wash and de-vein the kale and roughly chop

Bring your vegetable stock to the boil

Add the kale to the stock and simmer for one hour

Remove the kale and chop up finely and toss it in the oatmeal

Return to the pot

Gently warm the cream and add to the pot

Stir and simmer for 5 minutes

Red Lentil and Barley Soup

SERVES 6

What you will need:

1.5 litres of vegetable

1 cup (128g) of red lentils

1 cup pearl barley

4 carrots

1 onion

2 stalks of celery

2 teaspoons of chopped curly leaf parsley

What you will need to do:

Soak the pearl barley in cold water in the fridge overnight.

Rinse the red lentils and the barley and add to the stock. Bring to the boil, cover with a tight lid and begin simmering.

Peel, chop and dice the carrots and onion and add to the pot.

Remove the fibrous stringy bits from the celery and chop into small pieces and add to the pot and gently simmer for one hour.

Add the parsley just before serving

Tattie (Potato) Soup

SERVES 6-8

<u>What you will need</u>:

1.5 litres of vegetable stock

2lb (907g) of potatoes

2 onions

2 stalks of celery

Half a pint (250mls) of milk

Cup of curly leaf parsley

Tablespoon of flour

Splash of vegetable oil

<u>What you will need to do:</u>

Chop and dice the potatoes and onions, remove the fibrous stringy bits of the celery and chop into small pieces. Fry all these vegetables in the vegetable oil for 5 minutes.

Bring the stock to the boil and add the vegetables. Cover and simmer for 15 minutes then use a potato masher to mash.

Wash and chop the parsley.

Blend the flour with the milk and add to the pot to thicken. Stir well and add the parsley.

Tattie (Potato) and Leek Soup

SERVES 6-8

<u>What you will need</u>:

1.5 litres of vegetable stock

2lb (907g) potatoes

4 carrots

Small swede

2 leeks

Cup of curly leaf parsley

<u>What you need to do</u>:

Dice the potatoes, swede and 3 of the 4 carrots and add to the vegetable stock. Bring to the boil and simmer for 30 minutes.

Wash and cut the leek lengthways and then into small pieces and after the vegetables have simmered for 30 minutes, add the leek to the pot and simmer for a further 30 minutes.

Chop the curly leaf parsley and add it 5 minutes before serving.

Haricot Bean Soup

SERVES 6-8

What you will need:

1.5 litres of vegetable stock

340g (12oz) of pre-soaked haricot beans

2 onions

1 swede

450g (1lb) potatoes

1 tablespoon of flour

2 cups of milk

Half a cup of curly leaf parsley

What you will need to do:

Cut and dice the onions, swede and potatoes. Rinse the beans and add to the stock along with the diced vegetables. Bring to the boil and cover with a tight lid.

Simmer for 2 hours then force through a sieve and return to the pot. Mix the flour with a little of the milk and stir through the soup to thicken and then add the remaining milk.

Chop the parsley and just before serving, add to the pot.

Tomato Soup

SERVES 4

<u>What you will need</u>:

1 litre of vegetable stock

8 large or 10 medium blanched and skinned tomatoes

1 carrot

1 onion

2 tablespoons of sago

2 cups of milk

<u>What you will need to do</u>:

Cut up tomatoes, onion and carrot and add to the stock in a pot. Bring to the boil and add the sago. Simmer for 30 minutes.

Pass through a sieve, return to the pot and add the milk. Stir and heat, but do not boil.

Tomato, red pepper and lentil soup

SERVES 4

What you will need:

1 litre of vegetable stock

6 medium blanched and skinned tomatoes

2 red peppers

1 onion

2 cloves of garlic

2 teaspoons of olive oil

Half a cup (60g) of red lentils

What you will need to do:

Quarter the tomatoes, peppers and onion and put on a baking tray with the garlic

Mix the vegetables with the olive oil and roast in a medium oven for 15-20 minutes

Squeeze the roasted garlic from their skins and mix through the roasted vegetables. Remove the pepper skins

Rinse the lentils and add to the stock, bring to a simmer and simmer for 15 minutes, stirring occasionally

Add the vegetables and simmer for a further 10 minutes

Cream of mushroom soup

SERVES 4

What you will need:

1 litre of vegetable stock

500g of mixed mushrooms

50g of butter

1 onion

1 cup of crème fraiche

2 tablespoons of cream

What you will need to do:

Chop the mushrooms and the onion and fry in the butter until soft

Add to the stock and bring to a simmer then simmer for 20 minutes

Stir in the crème fraiche and simmer for a further 5 minutes

Blend (blitz) the soup and serve topped with a swirl of cream

Spicy parsnip soup

SERVES 4

<u>What you will need</u>:

1 litre of vegetable stock

1 cup of cream

Half a teaspoon of smoked paprika

Half a teaspoon of cumin

Half a teaspoon of chopped ginger

A quarter of a teaspoon of chili powder

6 large parsnips

1 onion

2 cloves of garlic

Knob of butter

Handful of coriander leaves

<u>What you will need to do</u>:

Peel and chop the parsnips and slice the garlic

Add to the butter in a frying pan and fry gently for a few minutes then add the chopped parsnip, the smoked paprika, cumin and chili powder

Fry gently for a few minutes then add to the vegetable stock and simmer for 30 minutes then stir in most of the cream

Blend (blitz) thoroughly until smooth and serve with a swirl of cream and with a garnish of chopped coriander leaves

Spicy vegetable soup

SERVES 4

What you will need:

1 litre of vegetable stock (you may need to add more later)

1 cup of milk

2 carrots

2 potatoes

2 small white turnips

1 parsnip

Half a cup of green lentils

1 onion

Half a teaspoon of cumin

Half a teaspoon of smoked paprika

Half a teaspoon of chili powder

Knob of butter

What you will need to do:

Peel and chop all the vegetables and fry off with the knob of butter then add to the vegetable stock and bring to a simmer. Add the spices and then simmer for 15 minutes

Rinse and then add the lentils and simmer for a further 30 minutes then add the milk and blend (blitz) thoroughly. Add more stock if required.

Potato and mint pea soup

SERVES 4

What you will need:

1 litre of vegetable stock

4 large potatoes

1 onion

3 cups of frozen peas

Knob of butter

2 tablespoons of cream

What you will need to do:

Peel and chop the onion and potatoes and fry off with the butter for 5 minutes

Add to the stock and bring to a simmer

Simmer for 20 minutes and then blend (blitz) thoroughly

Serve with a swirl of cream

Carrot and ginger soup

SERVES 4

What you will need:

1 litre of vegetable stock

6 carrots

1 onion

2 tablespoons of grated ginger

2 tablespoons of cream

Half a teaspoon of cayenne pepper

Knob of butter

What you will need to do:

Peel and chop the carrots and the onion and fry off for a couple of minutes with the butter then add the grated ginger and the cayenne pepper and fry for another minute.

Add to the stock and bring to a simmer then simmer for 15 minutes and then add the cream blend (blitz) thoroughly with the cream

SOUPS MADE WITH CHICKEN, MIXED FOWL OR TURKEY STOCK

Cock-a-leekie soup

SERVES 6-8

<u>What you will need</u>:

1.5 litres of chicken stock

1 small chicken

8 leeks

<u>What you will need to do:</u>

Bring the stock to a slow simmer and add the chicken to the pot.

Wash the leeks and prepare them by cutting off the root and about an inch from the top; remove the outer leaf and cut/split lengthwise then chop into one-inch lengths. Give the cut leeks a final rinse in cold water and add to the pot.

Simmer for one hour. Remove the chicken and take it off the bone and return the chicken meat to the pot. Remove from the heat and serve.

Feather Fowlie

SERVES 6-8

What you will need:

1.5 litres of chicken stock

Small chicken

2 slices of ham

Head of celery

2 onions

3 egg yolks

Half a cup of curly leaf parsley

A teaspoon of thyme

A dessertspoon of cream

What you need to do:

Joint the chicken and add it to the stock with the 2 slices of ham and bring to the boil. Simmer for 40 minutes. Remove the fibrous stringy bits from the celery and cut into small pieces. Chop and dice the onions, chop the parsley and add to the pot with the thyme and simmer for a further 20 minutes.

Remove the chicken and the ham Take the meat off the bone and cut into small pieces. Cut the ham into small pieces. Skim the grease from the stock. Remove the pot from the heat and stir in three whisked egg yolks and the dessertspoon of warmed cream. Add the chopped chicken and ham meat.

Chicken Soup

SERVES 4

What you will need:

1 litre of chicken stock

2 chicken legs

1 leek

2 large carrots

Half a cup (170g) of rice

Half a cup of curly leaf parsley

What you will need to do:

Put the chicken into the stock, bring to the boil and simmer for 10 minutes.

Cut and finely dice the carrot and add to the pot. Cut the leek lengthways and then cut into small pieces. Add to the pot with the rice and simmer for a further 30 minutes.

Add more stock if required.

Remove the chicken and take the meat off the bone and return to the pot.

Chop and add the parsley 5 minutes before serving.

Chunky Chicken and Vegetable soup

SERVES 6-8

<u>What you will need:</u>

1.5 litres of chicken stock

2 chicken legs

1 large leek

2 large carrots

1 potato

2 white turnips

1 parsnip

Half a small swede

Small head of broccoli

Half a cup of curly leaf parsley

<u>What you will need to do</u>:

Put the chicken into the stock, bring to the boil and simmer for 10 minutes.

Peel, rinse and cut up all of the vegetables and add to the pot. Simmer for a further 30 minutes.

Remove the chicken and take the meat off the bone and return to the pot.

Chop and add the parsley 5 minutes before serving.

Cream of Chicken Soup

SERVES 4

What you will need:

1 litre of chicken stock

2 chicken legs

1 large onion

1 medium leek

1 potato

2 stalks of celery

2 large carrots

Half a cup of flat leaf parsley

Knob of butter

Half a cup of cream

What you will need to do:

Put the chicken into the stock, bring to the boil and simmer for 10 minutes.

Cut the leek lengthways and then cut into small pieces. Peel and chop the onion. Remove the fibrous, stringy bits from the celery and chop. Peel and cube the potato.

Fry off all the vegetables with the butter for 5 minutes and then add to the stock. Simmer for a further 30 minutes.

Remove the chicken and then blend (blitz) the soup. Take off the heat and stir in the cream. Finely chop the chicken and add to the pot. Serve with a garnish of finely chopped parsley.

Chicken Broth

SERVES 8-10

What you will need:

2 litres of chicken stock

2 chicken legs

Quarter of a cup of split yellow peas

Quarter of a cup of split green peas

One cup of white rice

Quarter of a cup of red lentils

1 large leek

2 large carrots

Half a cup of curly leaf parsley

What you will need to do:

Pre-soak the peas in cold water overnight.

Put the chicken into the stock, bring to the boil and simmer for 10 minutes.

Cut and finely dice the carrot and add to the pot. Cut the leek lengthways and then cut into small pieces. Add to the pot with the pre-soaked peas and the rice and simmer for a further 40 minutes.

Remove the chicken and take the meat off the bone, chop finely and return to the pot. Chop and add the parsley 5 minutes before serving.

Turkey Broth

SERVES 6-8

<u>What you will need:</u>

1.5 litres of turkey stock

500g of cooked leftover holiday turkey

Quarter of a cup of split yellow peas

Quarter of a cup of split green peas

Half of a cup of pearl barley

Half of a cup of red lentils

1 large leek

2 large carrots

Half a cup of curly leaf parsley

<u>What you will need to do</u>:

Pre-soak the peas and the barley overnight in cold water

Peel and finely dice the carrots and wash and finely chop up the leek then add to the stock and bring to a rolling simmer. Rinse and add the peas and the barley and simmer for 10 minutes and then add the lentils. Simmer for a further 30 minutes and then add the leftover turkey that you have diced.

Chop the parsley and add just before serving

Spicy Turkey Soup

SERVES 4-6

<u>What you will need:</u>

1 litre of turkey stock

250g of leftover turkey

1 red pepper

1 large carrot

1 large potato

2 small white turnips

1 parsnip

Half a cup of green lentils

1 onion

Half a teaspoon of cumin

Half a teaspoon of smoked paprika

Half a teaspoon of chili powder

Knob of butter

<u>What you will need to do:</u>

Peel and dice all the vegetables and fry off with the knob of butter then add to the turkey stock and bring to a simmer. Add the spices and then simmer for 15 minutes

Rinse and add the green lentils and simmer for a further 30 minutes. Chop and add the turkey and simmer for another 5 minutes. Add more stock if required.

Duck Broth

SERVES 4-6

What you will need:

1 litre of mixed fowl or chicken stock

250g of leftover duck

2 brown onions

1 stick of celery

200g of mushrooms

Sprig of thyme

1 bay leaf

2 carrots

200mls of sherry

What you will need to do:

Peel and finely dice the onions and carrots. Remove fibrous bits from the celery stalk and finely dice. Finely dice the mushrooms.

Add the onions, carrots and celery to the stock. Add the thyme and the bay leaf and gently simmer for 15 minutes then add the mushrooms, the duck and the sherry and simmer for a further 5 minutes. Remove the sprig of thyme and the bay leaf.

SOUPS MADE WITH MEAT STOCK

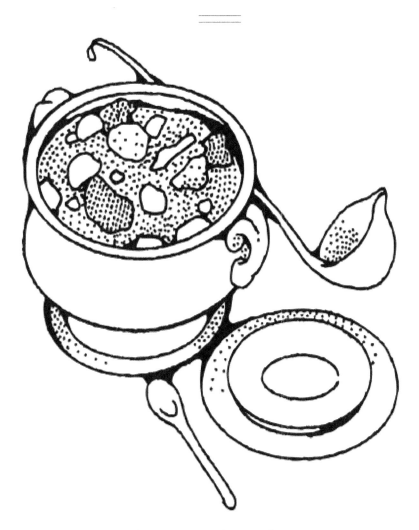

Beef, Pea and Barley Soup

SERVES 4-6

What you will need:

1 litre of rich beef stock

1 cup of pearl barley

1 onion

Half a cup of frozen green peas

More stock if required

<u>What you will need to do</u>:

Pre-soak the pearl barley in cold water overnight

Peel and finely dice the onion and add to the stock then add the barley and simmer for 30 minutes

Add more stock if required

Add the peas and simmer for a further 5 minutes

Lamb and Cabbage Soup

SERVES 4-6

<u>What you will need:</u>

1 litre of the vegetable and lamb stock

Leftover lamb

2 stalks of celery

A quarter of a green cabbage

2 tomatoes

1 leek

2 carrots

<u>What you need to do:</u>

Remove the fibrous, stringy bits from the celery and finely dice.

Chop up the cabbage and peel and finely dice the carrots. Roughly chop the tomatoes and wash and chop the leek

Add everything to the stock and simmer for 15 minutes then add the leftover lamb

Scotch Broth

SERVES 6 - 8

What you will need:

1.5 litres of the vegetable and lamb stock

The breast of lamb used for the stock

Pre-soaked broth mixture – (64g of pearl barley, 64g of yellow split peas and 64g of green split peas)

2 large onions

4 large carrots

2 white turnips

Small swede

A head of celery

A cup of chopped curly leaf parsley (128g)

What you need to do:

Add the pre-soaked broth mix to the stock and bring to a slow boil. Simmer for forty minutes, stirring occasionally.

Chop and dice the onions, carrots, turnips and celery and add to the pot. Continue to simmer for a further fifteen minutes then add most of the parsley and the lamb and simmer for a further five minutes. Take off the heat and chop the lamb and add to the pot with the remaining parsley.

Skink

SERVES 6-8

<u>What you will need:</u>

1.5 litres of rich beef stock

The shin and/or the brisket used to make the stock

4 large carrots

1 small swede

2 leeks

Head of celery

2 onions

Half of a savoy cabbage

<u>What you need to do:</u>

Bring stock to a slow simmer

Chop and dice the carrots, swede and onions

Chop and cut up the celery

Cut the cabbage and the leeks and chop into small pieces

Add all of the prepared vegetables to the stock and simmer for 30 minutes.

Cut the shin and/or brisket into small cubes and add to the pot.

Switch off and allow the residual heat to warm through the beef.

This is a thick soup, but you can add more stock if you want it a little thinner.

Oxtail Soup

SERVES 4

What you will need:

1 litre of your oxtail stock

8 pieces of the pre-cooked oxtail used to make your stock

3 carrots

1 swede

2 white turnips

1 large onion

Tablespoon of vegetable oil

What you will need to do:

Chop and dice the carrots, swede, turnips and onion and fry off for a few minutes in the vegetable oil.

Bring the stock to a slow simmer, add the vegetables and simmer for 30 minutes.

Add the oxtails to the soup to warm through.

Serve 2 portions of the oxtails with each portion of soup (this was my wee granny's preferred way to serve the oxtails, as sucking out the meat from the bones was awesome, but you can fork the meat out of the bones and add it to the soup if you prefer.)

SOUPS MADE WITH HAM STOCK

Red Lentil and Tomato Soup

SERVES 4

What you will need:

A third of a litre of slightly salted water

1 litre of ham stock

1 cup (128g) of red lentils

4 carrots

1 onion

2 stalks of celery

4 large fresh tomatoes

What you will need to do:

Bring the salted water to the boil

Rinse the red lentils and add to the water. Cover and simmer for 20 minutes stirring frequently so as not to burn on the bottom. Add more boiling water if required.

Peel, chop and dice the carrots, onion and the tomatoes.

Remove the fibrous stringy bits from the celery and chop into small pieces.

In a separate pot, bring the stock to the boil, add all of the vegetables and simmer for 20 minutes.

After the lentils have simmered for 20 minutes leave to one side.

Once the vegetables have simmered in the stock for 20 minutes, use a potato masher to roughly mash them and then add the lentils. Stir thoroughly and simmer for a further 10 minutes.

Dried Pea and Ham Soup

SERVES 4

What you will need:

1 litre of ham stock

225g (8oz) of pre-soaked dried green peas

1 onion

1 small white turnip

Half a cup of curly leaf parsley

Teaspoon of vegetable oil

What you will need to do:

Chop and dice the onion, carrot and turnip and fry gently in the oil then add to the stock with the peas. Bring to the boil, cover and simmer for 2 hours.

Chop the parsley for garnish

Cream of Ham and Vegetable Soup

SERVES 4

What you will need:

1 litre of ham stock

Leftover ham

1 celery stalk

4 red potatoes

1 red onion

1 carrot

1 tin of evaporated milk

Knob of butter

Tablespoon of flour

What you will need to do:

Peel and finely dice the potatoes, onion and carrot

Remove the fibrous, stringy bits from the celery and finely dice

Dust all of the vegetables in the flour and gently fry off in the butter then add to the broth and simmer for 20 minutes

Add the evaporated milk and stir through until completely mixed and then add the leftover ham and simmer for a further 5 minutes

Ham and Potato Soup

SERVES 4

What you will need:

1 litre of ham stock

Leftover ham

2 celery stalks

4 red potatoes

1 red onion

1 carrot

1 parsnip

2 tablespoons of cream

1 sprig of thyme

1 bay leaf

Knob of butter

What you will need to do:

Peel and cube the potatoes, carrot, parsnip and onions. Remove the fibrous, stringy bits from the celery and chop.

Fry all of the vegetable in the butter for 5 minutes and add to the stock along with the sprig of thyme and the bay leaf. Simmer for 20 minutes and then remove half of the vegetables.

Remove the thyme and the bay leaf

Blend (blitz) the remaining vegetables with the stock and then return the remaining vegetables to the pot along with the leftover ham and stir in the cream

SOUPS MADE WITH FISH STOCK

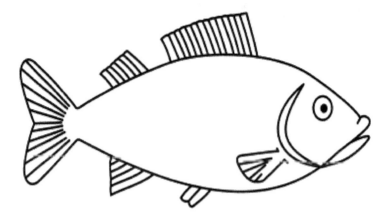

Cullen Skink

SERVES 4-6

<u>What you will need</u>

<u>(There is no need to use fish stock with this recipe)</u>

2 large pieces of smoked haddock (undyed)

1 onion

2 knobs of butter

2 cups of milk

1 cup of cream

4 potatoes

1 bay leaf

Half a cup of parsley

<u>What you will need to do</u>

Put the haddock in a large pan and cover with the milk (add more milk if needed to just cover the fish. Add the bay leaf and bring to a gentle simmer and then simmer for 10 minutes

Peel and chop the onion and fry until soft in the butter

Remove the fish from the pan and put to the side until later

Peel and cube the potatoes and add to the milk liquor then simmer until potatoes are cooked then remove the bay leaf, add the cream and onions. Chop the parsley and add. Simmer for a further minute

Shell Fish Soup

SERVES 4-6

What you will need:

1 litre of rich shellfish stock

100g Clams

100g Cockles

100g Mussels

4 Razor fish

100g King prawns

1 cup of milk

Knob of butter

Half a cup of oatmeal

What you will need to do:

Put all the shellfish, except the prawns, in a pot, cover with water and bring to the boil. Simmer until cooked and remove any where the shells have remained closed.

Shell and de-vein the king prawns.

Remove all the shellfish and remove from the shells. Cut up the razor fish and then add the clams, mussels and razor fish to your prepared stock. Bring back to a gentle simmer, add the half cup of oatmeal, the knob of butter and the cup of milk. After five minutes add the de-shelled and de-veined prawns. Switch off the heat, cover and let stand until the prawns cook in the residual heat.

Partan Bree (Crab Soup)

SERVES 4-6

<u>What you will need</u>

Half a litre of shellfish stock

1 large crab

A quarter of a cup of rice

Two and a half cups of milk

Three quarters of a cup of cream

One tablespoon of chives

<u>What you will need to do</u>

Cook the crab and remove the meat, separating the brown and white meat

Cook the rice in the stock and the milk, add the brown meat and blend (blitz)

Add the white meat and mix through the cream

Garnish with chopped chives

FISH DISHES

SCOTLAND IS RENOWNED for its abundance of fish. My wee granny most commonly cooked with herrings, salmon, trout, whiting, haddock, mackerel and cod. Many Scottish fish dishes are served with a traditional egg sauce.

Fish is low in saturated fat and low in the bad omega-6 fatty acids, high in protein and bursts with flavour. Oily fish such as mackerel and salmon are high in omega-3 fatty acids which are very good for the body.

Always ensure your fish is fresh by checking that the eyes are clear. If in doubt, place your fish in water and, if it floats, then it is fresh.

Some of these fish dish recipes date back to the 1800s and were popular during the 1900s and are still used in Scotland even today.

Please note that lard or dripping has been replaced by vegetable oil or butter.

Egg Sauce

HARD BOIL AND CHOP 2 eggs. Mix 2 tablespoons of cornflour (corn starch) with 2 cups (500ml) of cold milk. Once it is smooth add 100g of butter, salt and freshly ground black pepper. Bring to the boil, stirring continuously for one minute. Blend in half a teaspoon of lemon juice, 2 teaspoons of dill and the chopped eggs.

Baked Cod

SERVES 4

What you will need:

A cup of basic fish stock

4 cod loins

12 cherry tomatoes

2 tablespoons of flat leaf parsley

The juice of one lemon

What you will need to do:

Put the cod loins and the cherry tomatoes in an oven proof dish and cover with the fish stock. Add the lemon juice. Place in a preheated moderate oven and bake for twenty minutes.

Garnish with the parsley.

Cabbie Claw version one

SERVES 4-6

What you will need:

1lb cod fillets

1lb potatoes

2oz butter

1 dessertspoon of cornflour

Half a teaspoon of dried mustard

1 hard-boiled egg

3oz grated cheese

Half a pint of milk

Salt and pepper

What you will need to do:

Boil the potatoes until cooked then slice them

Put the majority of the milk, butter, salt and pepper into a frying pan and add the cod. Bring to a slow boil and simmer gently for 6 or 7 minutes or until the fish is cooked through.

Mix the cornflour with the remaining milk and add the mustard. Mix thoroughly and add to the pan.

Shake gently to mix through and continue shaking gently until the sauce thickens. Turn out into a casserole dish.

Place the sliced potatoes on top, add the grated cheese and put in a pre-heated hot oven for 10 minutes.

Cabbie Claw version two

SERVES 4-6

<u>What you will need</u>:

200mls of basic fish stock

1lb cod fillets

Half a cup of curly leaf parsley

Quarter of an inch of grated horseradish

900g (1lb) potatoes

1 dessertspoon of cornflour

<u>What you will need to do</u>:

Boil the potatoes, cool and slice

Finely chop the parsley

Mix the cornflour with a little of the cold fish stock

Bring the remaining fish stock to the boil and reduce the heat to a gentle simmer. Add the cod and gently simmer for 5 minutes and then add the chopped parsley and the grated horseradish. Simmer for a further 5 minutes and then gently add the cornflour and thicken the stock by gently stirring (trying not to break up the cod.).

Turn out into a casserole dish and layer the potatoes on top.

Serve with egg sauce.

Traditional Whiting

SERVES 4

What you will need:

2 cups of basic fish stock

8 whiting fillets

2 tablespoons of flour

3 knobs of butter

2 tablespoons of cream

2 tablespoons of chopped chives

Half a cup of chopped parsley

What you will need to do:

Ensure your fillets are dry and rub each of them with flour

Add the knobs of butter to a large frying pan, melt and add the fish and gently sauté them very slowly for 2 minutes. DO NOT brown them.

Ensure the chives and the parsley are very finely chopped and put in a bowl with the fish stock and mix thoroughly then add to the pan.

Bring to a gentle simmer and simmer for 2 or 3 minutes.

Try not to break them up when you lift them out. 2 fillets per portion

Curled Whiting

SERVES 4

What you will need:

4 whole whiting with eyes removed

Half a cup of breadcrumbs

50g of melted butter

Salt and pepper

Third of a cup of chopped curly leaf parsley

Four lemon wedges

What you will need to do:

Curl each of the fish and put the tail through the eye socket.

Place in a greased tin and brush over the melted butter.

Season with the salt and pepper and sprinkle over with the breadcrumbs

Put in a preheated moderate oven and bake for 30 minutes

Garnish with the chopped parsley and the lemon wedges

Whiting Pudding

SERVES 4

What you will need:

4 whole whiting

900g of potatoes (2lbs)

Half a pint (250mls) of milk

Salt and pepper

100g of butter

What you will need to do:

Boil the fish in the milk for 15 minutes

Boil the potatoes until cooked

Remove, debone and deskin

Mash the fish

Strain the milk and add 3 tablespoons to the cooked potatoes along with half of the butter. Mash and mix in the fish.

Mash the potato and fish mix to an oven proof dish and smooth out with a knife. Add the remaining butter in small dollops across the top.

Brown in a moderate oven.

Serve with egg sauce.

Traditional Herrings

SERVES 4

<u>What you will need:</u>

8 fresh boned herring fillets (flattened carefully)

Salt and pepper

2 cups of oatmeal

Vegetable oil

<u>What you will need to do:</u>

Ensure the herring fillets are dry

Season with salt and pepper

Put oatmeal on a large plate and thoroughly coat each fillet with the oatmeal

Put vegetable oil in a large frying pan and heat until very hot

Add the herring and brown them until crisp on both sides

Lay on paper to drain the excess oil and serve immediately

Potted Herring

SERVES 6

<u>What you will need:</u>

12 fresh boned herring fillets

Salt and pepper

12 black peppercorns

2 bay leaves

Half a cup of vinegar

Half a cup of water

<u>What you will need to do:</u>

Season each fillet with salt and pepper

Mix the half cup of vinegar with the half cup of water

Roll each fillet inside out starting from the tail end

Pack them side by side in a small pie dish and just cover with the vinegar and water mix

Add the 12 peppercorns and 2 bay leaves and bake in a preheated moderate oven

Crappit Heids (stuffed heads) (version one)

SERVES 8

<u>What you will need</u>:

0.5 litres of basic fish stock

8 haddock heads

One cup of oatmeal

100g of butter

2 onions

One cup of white crab meat

2 anchovies

Chopped cooked yolk of 2 eggs

1 beaten egg

One cup of breadcrumbs

Salt and pepper

<u>What you will need to do</u>:

Chop and dice the onions and mix through the oatmeal. Add the anchovies, the crabmeat and the breadcrumbs and mix thoroughly. Break up the butter and add. Bind the mixture with the beaten egg and gently fold in the chopped egg yolks.

Use the mixture to stuff the 8 haddock heads and place them on end on the bottom of a large buttered stew pan. Cover with the fish stock, bring to the boil and simmer for 30 minutes.

Crappit Heids (stuffed heads) (version two)

SERVES 8

<u>What you will need</u>:

0.5 litres of basic fish stock

8 haddock heads

One cup of haddock livers

One cup of oatmeal

Half a cup of milk

Salt and pepper

<u>What you will need to do</u>:

Chop the livers and mix with the oatmeal. Bind with the milk. Season with salt and pepper.

Stuff the heads with the mixture and place the heads on end on the bottom of a large stew pot. Cover with the fish stock. Bring to the boil and simmer for 30 minutes.

Tatties and Herring

SERVES 4

What you will need:

0.5 litres of basic fish stock

900g (2lbs) potatoes

8 salt herring fillets

What you will need to do:

Peel and dice the potatoes

Put in a large pot and cover with the fish stock.

Lay the salt herring fillets on top.

Bring to a slow boil and gently simmer on a very low heat for minutes.

Spiced Salmon

SERVES 4

What you will need:

4 salmon fillets

28g of salt

28g of black peppercorns

28g of cinnamon

One-pint (500mls) Vinegar

One pint of water

What you will need to do:

Mix the water and vinegar and add the salt, peppercorns and cinnamon. Add the salmon fillets and bring to the boil. Simmer for 10 minutes.

Remove the salmon and allow to cool then pack them in a deep dish and cover completely with the cooled cooking liquor. Cover so the dish is airtight. Serve with egg sauce.

Salmon Fritters

SERVES 4

What you will need:

4 cooked salmon fillets

450g (1lb) of boiled potatoes

Yolk of one egg

4 hard-boiled eggs

2 tablespoons of cream

Vegetable oil

Salt and pepper

What you will need to do:

Mash the boiled potatoes and mix in the egg yolk and the cream. Season with salt and pepper.

Flake the cooked salmon fillets through the mashed potatoes and mix thoroughly.

Mould into small fritters and fry in vegetable oil until golden on both sides.

Each portion to be served with a quartered hard-boiled egg.

Friar's Trout in Sauce

SERVES 4

What you will need:

Half a litre of basic fish stock

4 cleaned and gutted whole trout

2 onions

4 cloves

4 teaspoons of black peppercorns

2 teaspoons of salt

2 glasses of white wine

4 anchovies

Juice of 1 lemon

One teaspoon of cayenne pepper

1 dessertspoon of cornflour

100g butter

What you will need to do:

Mix the peppercorns, salt and cayenne pepper together and divide into 4 portions. Use one portion per trout and rub the mix inside the belly of the fish. Place the fish in a stew pan and cover with the stock.

Chop and dice the onions and add to the pot. Add the 4 cloves.

Bring to the boil and gently simmer for 5 minutes and then add the 2 glasses of wine and the 4 anchovies. Add the lemon juice.

Gently simmer for 20 minutes then gently remove the trout and place in a casserole dish.

Thicken the stock with cornflour and add the butter. Pour the stock over the trout and serve hot.

Potted Salmon

SERVES 4

What you will need:

4 fillets of salmon

The juice and zest of 1 lemon

1 teaspoon of chopped dill

1 teaspoon of chopped flat parsley

1 teaspoon of cayenne pepper

200g of unsalted butter

Salt and pepper

What you will need to do:

Flake the salmon fillets and put in a bowl.

Add the lemon juice and zest, the dill and the parsley and mix. Taste and add salt and pepper to season...

Pour in three quarters of the melted butter and mix thoroughly.

Taste again and add more seasoning if required.

Divide the salmon mix between 4 teacups and smooth the tops before brushing on the remaining butter.

Chill in the fridge for 2 hours before serving.

Serve with toasted bread.

Leek and Mackerel Patties

SERVES 4

What you will need:

450g (1lb) potatoes

2 leeks

1 tablespoon of capers

4 mackerel fillets

100g of butter

Half a cup of milk

Salt and pepper

Vegetable oil

What you will need to do:

Boil the potatoes in salted water and mash with the butter

Cut the leeks up very small and poach to soften in the milk season with the salt and pepper.

Add the mackerel to the milk and leeks and continue poaching until the fish is cooked through. When cooked, drain then flake the mackerel with a fork and add to the mashed potatoes. Mix thoroughly and make into small patties.

Fry the patties in the vegetable oil until golden on both sides.

Serve with egg sauce.

Crispy Skinned Mackerel

SERVES 4

What you will need:

4 butterflied mackerel skin on

1 spring onion

1 lemon

Salt and pepper

What you will need to do:

Heat a frying pan until piping hot and add the mackerel skin down. Season with salt and pepper and grate the zest of the lemon over it. Fry until the skin side is dark brown – pressing down with a fish slice (for about 3 minutes) then flip over and fry for a few seconds on the other side.

Trim and finely slice the spring onions and sprinkle over the cooked fish.

Serve with buttered toast.

Crappit Cod (stuffed cod)

SERVES 6-8

What you will need:

Half a litre of basic fish stock

One whole cod, cleaned, descaled and gutted

The meat from one cooked crab

4 anchovies

2 cooked egg yolks

2 eggs

1 cup of oatmeal

100g of butter

Half a cup of flat leaf parsley

What you will need to do:

Mix the crab meat, the anchovies, the oatmeal, the egg yolks, the butter and the parsley thoroughly together and stuff it into the belly of the cod.

Put the cod in a fish bath and cover with the fish stock. Cover and bake in a moderate oven for one hour.

Add additional seasoning if required.

Serve with egg sauce.

John Dory with Cockles, Spinach and Egg Sauce

SERVES 6

What you will need:

6 John Dory fillets

300g of cockles

2 tablespoons of butter

300g of baby spinach

Salt and pepper

2 tablespoons of olive oil

What you will need to do:

Rub the John Dory in half of the olive oil and season with the salt and pepper then steam the fish for approximately 10 minutes

Cook the cockles in seasoned boiling water that has had the remaining olive oil added until the shells all open (2 or 3 minutes will do)

Sauté the spinach in butter (2 minutes should do it)

Serve the fish on top of the spinach. Drain the cockles and pour over the fish.

Serve with egg sauce.

SIDE DISHES

MY WEE GRANNY'S FULL TABLE

Anchovy Potatoes

WHAT YOU WILL NEED:

500g of potatoes

4 anchovy fillets

1 tablespoon of flat leafed parsley

1 tablespoon of butter

2 tablespoons of cream

Salt and pepper

1 teaspoon of extra virgin olive oil

1 teaspoon of lemon juice

What you will need to do:

Peel and boil the potatoes in salted water until soft

Grind the anchovies and mix in the olive oil, the lemon juice and the parsley

Drain the potatoes, add the butter and the cream and roughly mash and then add the anchovy mix and blend in thoroughly

Colcannon

SERVES 6

What you will need:

2 cabbages

3 carrots

8 potatoes

2 white turnips

2 shallots

2 teaspoons of vinegar

2 tablespoons of butter

Black pepper

Salt

What you will need to do:

Cut and dice the shallots and cook in the vinegar until soft.

Cut and dice all of the other vegetables. Boil the cabbage separately in salted water. Boil the potatoes, carrots and turnips together in salted water and when cooked, mash and boil in salted water until cooked. Drain and mash. Chop up the cooked cabbage and add to the other vegetables and mix through the butter with the shallots. Season with black pepper.

Kailkenny

SERVES 4

What you will need:

450g of potatoes

450g of cabbage

Half a cup of cream

Black pepper

Salt

What you will need to do:

Cut and dice the cabbage and potatoes and boil in salted water. When cooked, drain and thoroughly mash. Mix in the cream and season with pepper.

Rumbledethumps

SERVES 4-6

What you will need:

900g of potatoes

900g of cabbage

2 onions

200g of grated cheese

2 tablespoons of butter

Bunch of chives

Black pepper

Salt

What you will need to do:

Cut and dice the potatoes, cabbage and onions and boil in salted water. When cooked, mash with the butter and the pepper. Cut up the chives and mix through.

Put in a pie dish and cover with the grated cheese. Brown in the oven.

Potato fritters

SERVES 4

What you will need:

6 kidney potatoes

2 rashers of lean bacon

1 tablespoon of fine breadcrumbs

2 tablespoons of butter

Black pepper

Salt

What you will need to do:

Part boil the potatoes and slice

Fry the bacon and finely chop.

Beat up the eggs and mix in the breadcrumbs and the chopped bacon and dip the sliced potatoes in the egg mixture.

Fry in melted butter until golden brown on each side.

Season with salt and pepper.

Sautéed Baby Potatoes with Spring Onions

WHAT YOU WILL NEED:

500g of baby potatoes (the newer the better)

4 spring onions

75g of butter

Salt and pepper

What you will need to do:

Part boil the potatoes in salted water and drain

Finely chop the spring onions and gently mix half of them through the potatoes

Melt the butter in a frying pan and add the potato and spring onion mix. Season with pepper

Gently fry, turning so the potatoes don't stick, for a further 15 minutes, or until browned

Serve garnished with the remaining spring onions

Beetroot Relish

WHAT YOU WILL NEED:

8 baby beetroot

2 shallots

1 teaspoon of sugar

1 teaspoon of lime juice

1 teaspoon of finely chopped flat leafed parsley

1 teaspoon of malt vinegar

What you will need to do:

Scrub and wrap the beetroot in foil and bake in a moderate to hot oven for 45 minutes. When cooked, peel and dice and put in a bowl.

Finely dice the shallots and add to the bowl along with the parsley, sugar, lime juice and vinegar. Mix thoroughly.

Purried Neeps

SERVES 6

<u>What you will need</u>:

1 swede

6 white turnips

Half a teaspoon of grated ginger

2 tablespoons of butter

Salt and white pepper

<u>What you will need to do</u>:

Cut and dice the swede and the turnips and boil in salted water. When cooked, mash with the butter and the grated ginger. Season with white pepper.

Stewed Onions

WHAT YOU WILL NEED

12 medium onions

Half a litre of rich beef stock

Tablespoon of cornflour

Teaspoon of mushroom catsup

What you will need to do:

Peel the onions and add them to the stock. Boil and simmer for 1 hour. Thicken with cornflour and add the mushroom catsup.

Clapshot

SERVES 6

What you will need:

900g of potatoes

900g of turnips

A bunch of chives

2 tablespoons of butter

Black pepper

Salt

What you will need to do:

Cut and dice the potatoes and turnips and boil in salted water, when cooked, drain and mash with the butter. Chop the chives and mix through with the pepper.

Skirlie

WHAT YOU WILL NEED:

50g of Butter

1 onion

125g of oatmeal

What you will need to do:

Roughly chop the onion. Add the butter and the onion to a pan and gently fry until the onions change colour. Add the oatmeal and thoroughly mix through. Cook for approximately 10 minutes and season with salt and pepper.

Whisky Cauliflower Cheese

WHAT YOU WILL NEED:

One cauliflower

200g of mushrooms

Half a yellow bell pepper

300mls of cream

400g of strong grated cheese

6 tablespoons of whisky

1 tablespoon of oatmeal

Salt and pepper

One cauliflower

What you will need to do:

Cut the cauliflower into florets and cook in simmering water for approximately five minutes then drain and place in an ovenproof dish.

Chop the mushrooms and the yellow pepper and mix through the cauliflower

Meantime, gently warm through the cream in a saucepan and then add most of the grated cheese. Stir until the cheese melts and then remove from the heat and stir in the whisky and the oatmeal. Season with salt and pepper and pour over the cauliflower mix. Sprinkle the remaining cheese on top.

Bake in a medium oven (170 degrees C) for approximately 45 minutes.

Egg, Cheese and Veggie Spoons

SERVED ON THE SIDE in dessert spoons

<u>What you will need:</u>

4 eggs

200g of strong grated cheese

200g of broccoli florets

200g of cauliflower florets

1 leek

100g of green beans

300mls of single cream

Salt and pepper

<u>What you will need to do:</u>

Finely slice the leeks and chop the green beans then mix with the broccoli and cauliflower. Cook in salted water for 10 minutes then add to a non-stick oven-proof dish.

Meantime, gently warm through the cream and add most of the cheese. Season with salt and pepper. When the cheese has melted, pour over the vegetable mix. Top with the remaining cheese and bake in a moderate oven (170 degrees C) for 45 minutes.

Heap dessert spoons with the mixture and serve on the side.

POULTRY

DUCK AND GOOSE SHOULD be served rare.

Chicken, pheasant, partridges and red grouse should be cooked through and not pink.

Wood grouse should be *just* cooked – neither over nor under done.

Roast Grouse

SERVES 4-6

What you will need:

2 young hen wood grouse

4 rashers of bacon

2 tablespoons of butter

A teaspoon of lemon juice

Salt and pepper

A half cup of cranberries

1 tablespoon of flour

What you will need to do:

Work the butter and the lemon juice over and inside the birds then stuff with the cranberries. Wrap the bacon around the birds and cover with greaseproof paper.

Roast in a preheated oven (moderate to hot) 30 minutes... Remove the greaseproof paper and the bacon, dust with the flour and brown in a buttered pan.

Stoved Howtowdie

SERVES 4-6

<u>What you will need</u>:

500mls of chicken stock

1 chicken

250g of the stuffing of your choice

3 tablespoons of butter

10 button onions

6 eggs

Half a cup of chopped chicken livers

1 cup of chopped spinach

<u>What you will need to do</u>:

Stuff the bird with the stuffing of your choice. Place it in a stew pot that has a tight-fitting lid along with the stock, the chicken livers, the onions and the butter.

Simmer gently for 1 hour. When ready mash down the livers to thicken the stock. Poach the eggs and wilt the spinach.

Serve with the poached eggs on a bed of spinach.

Whisky Chicken

SERVES 4

What you will need:

150mls of chicken stock

3 tablespoons of single malt whisky

4 chicken breasts, boned and skinned

250mls of double cream

125g of butter

25g of flaked almonds

4 apples

Tablespoon of flour

What you will need to do:

Dust the chicken with the flour. Melt half the butter in a frying pan and fry the breasts until they are golden brown

Sprinkle the whisky over the breasts, add the chicken stock, cover and simmer for ten minutes. 180 degrees centigrade

Peel the apples and cut thickly into slices and, without stirring, cook in the remaining butter until partly soft.

Remove the breasts and add gently stir in the cream without boiling. Taste and add more whisky if required. Add the almonds and pour the sauce over the chicken and garnish with the sliced apples.

Roastit Bubbly-Jock

SERVES 6

What you will need:

3.5kg (8lb) turkey

One cup of basic breadcrumb stuffing

300g of chicken livers

250g of sausage meat.

60g of melted butter

Tablespoon of redcurrant jelly

2 cups of warm water

What you will need to do:

Preheat the oven to 180 degrees centigrade

To the basic stuffing mix, add half of the chicken livers and the sausage meat and mix thoroughly.

Stuff the turkey cavity with the stuffing mix and ensure it is well sealed by skewering the opening.

Put the turkey in a deep dish, brush on the melted butter and add the warm water and the remaining chicken livers

Put the turkey in the oven uncovered for 20 minutes then cover with foil. Roast for 20 minutes per pound plus an additional 20 minutes.

When cooked, allow to stand for 10 minutes, meantime place the pan juices and the livers into a pan and boil vigorously until it reduces by half and add the redcurrant jelly and use as the sauce for the turkey.

Chicken Heather

SERVES 4

What you will need:

1 chicken

Half a cup of melted butter

125g of clear heather honey

100g of French mustard

1 clove of chopped garlic

Quarter of a teaspoon of turmeric powder

Quarter of a teaspoon of cumin powder

Quarter of a teaspoon of chili

What you will need to do:

Preheat the oven to 190 degrees centigrade

Place the chicken in an ovenproof dish

Mix all the other ingredients together and pour over the chicken. Cover and roast for 1 hour. Uncover and thoroughly baste the chicken with the juices and roast uncovered for another 30 minutes.

Pan Fried Pigeon

SERVES 4

<u>What you will need</u>:

4 skinned pigeon breasts

250mls of chicken stock

2 tablespoons of red wine 1 onion

2 sticks of celery

4 slices of black pudding

1 tablespoon of butter

1 teaspoon of redcurrant jelly

<u>What you will need to do</u>:

Joint the pigeons

Melt the butter in a pan and add the pigeon breasts. Fry for 2 minutes on each side then remove from the pan and rest.

Deglaze the pan with the stock and the wine and add the redcurrant jelly. Reduce by half.

Meantime fry the black pudding and serve with the pigeon and the sauce.

Pheasant with Cider and Bacon

SERVES 6

What you will need:

2 pheasants

100g of bacon

2 apples

2 sticks of celery

Tablespoon of butter

4 sage leaves

500mls of cider

300mls of chicken stock

1 savoy cabbage

100mls of cream

Salt and pepper

What you will need to do:

Preheat the oven to 170 degrees centigrade

Melt the butter in a frying pan, season the birds and brown in the pan.

Put the birds in an ovenproof dish.

Chop the bacon and dice the onion. Cut up the celery (after removing the fibrous stringy bits) and cut up the sage. Add all of these ingredients to the pan and fry gently for 10 minutes, remove excess fat.

Cut up the apples and place over the pheasants.

Chop the cabbage and add to the dish with the stock and the cider. Cover and put in the oven for 25 minutes then mix through the cream.

Pot Roast Late Season Grouse with Wild Mushrooms

SERVES 8

What you will need:

2 grouse

6 shallots

2 carrots

8 chestnut mushrooms

6 cloves of garlic

1 cup of cream

1 pint of chicken stock

40mls of brandy

2 teaspoons of wholegrain mustard

Salt and pepper

What you will need to do:

Dry the birds and season with the salt and pepper. Brown in a frying pan with the butter and put in a large stew pot.

Chop the carrots, garlic, mushrooms and shallots and add to the pot. Pour over the stock and half of the brandy. Half cover with a lid and bring to the boil then gently simmer for 25 minutes.

Remove the birds and further reduce the stock. Add the cream and the mustard and reduce still further. Add additional salt and pepper if required. At the last minute, add the remaining brandy.

GAME AND OTHER MEAT DISHES

Calf's Liver

WHAT YOU WILL NEED:

4 slices of calf's liver

A tablespoon of flour

Salt and pepper

A tablespoon of butter

What you need to do:

You don't have to do much. Simply dry the liver and lightly dust with flour seasoned with the salt and pepper.

Melt the butter in a hot pan and flash fry the liver... only 15 seconds on each side... and, that's it. It's served pink. Don't overcook it. Under is better than over.

Pickled Pork

PICKLED PORK IS USUALLY used as a seasoning meat, but you can also pickle leg, rump or shoulder and then roast. This recipe uses either pork hocks or belly pork.

What you will need:

4 pork hocks or 1200g of belly pork

1 and a half litres of cold water

1 litre of vinegar

4 teaspoons of black peppercorns

3 bay leaves

4 teaspoons of whole coriander seeds

30g of sugar

400g of salt

2 onions

What you will need to do:

Wash the pork and put in a large stew pot with all of the ingredients except the pork. Bring to a rapid boil and simmer for 10 minutes. Skim off any scum that forms on the top. Rapidly cool the liquor by sitting the pot in iced water.

Trim the pork of excess fat and place in a larger airtight container. Pour over the cooled liquor ensuring the pork is fully submerged. Keep in the fridge for 3 days.

Once pickled and cured, the pork can be cut up and used as a seasoning for other dishes (for example – see Kingdom of Fife Pie recipe) or can be roasted.

Square (Lorne) Sausage

WHAT YOU WILL NEED:

450g of minced beef

450g of minced pork

50g of minced pork fat

150g of pin head rusk

Half a cup of cold water

2 teaspoons of salt

One and a half teaspoons of black pepper

One and a half teaspoons of ground coriander

Half a teaspoon of grated nutmeg

What you will need to do:

Combine the minced beef, minced pork and minced pork fat.

Mix the salt, pepper, coriander and nutmeg and mix thoroughly through the meat. Add the water and mix through once more then mix in the rusk.

When fully mixed, put in a loaf tin and cover. Put in the fridge for 24 hours, turn out of the tin and slice.

Fry the slices for 2 to 3 minutes on each side.

(Can also be used for stovies)

Aberdeen Sausage

WHAT YOU WILL NEED:

450g of Lorne sausage meat

450g of minced beef

4 rashers of bacon

1 cup of fresh breadcrumbs

1 beaten egg

Salt and pepper

Half a cup of toasted breadcrumbs

What you will need to do:

Chop the bacon finely.

Mix together the sausage meat, the minced beef, the bacon the cup of fresh breadcrumbs. Season with the salt and pepper and bind with the beaten egg.

Mould the mixture into a roll and wrap it in a floured muslin cloth then boil for 1 and a half hours.

Remove from the cloth and roll in the toasted breadcrumbs.

Serve cold.

Roast Haunch of Venison

SERVES 6

Preparation: season the venison by rubbing a mix of salt and black pepper all over then soak it for 6 hours in a mix of 500mls of claret or port and the juice of 3 lemons. Turn and baste frequently.

What you will need:

1 haunch (back leg) of venison around 3kg in weight

2 tablespoons of butter

1 teaspoon of walnut catsup

1 tablespoon of flou500mls of rich beef stock

What you will need to do:

Once you have marinated the meat, strain the liquor.

Melt the butter and rub into the haunch.

Cover with greaseproof paper and roast in an oven pre-heated to 220 degrees centigrade for 20 minutes and then turn the oven down to 150 degrees centigrade and roast for 10 minutes per half a kg to serve rare. 15 minutes before it is ready, remove the greaseproof paper, baste thoroughly and dredge lightly with flour until it froths, and browns then add the stock and the catsup ketchup to the roasting pan and leave in the oven for the remaining 15 minus.

Venison Collops

SERVES 6

<u>What you will need</u>:

Haunch, neck or loin of venison cut into slices

500mls of rich meat stock thickened with flour and butter

200mls of claret

Tablespoon of butter

<u>What you will need to do</u>:

Bring the stock to a gentle boil and add the claret.

Fry the collops in butter until lightly browned on both sides

Pour the sauce over the collops and serve

Hare Casserole

SERVES 4

What you will need:

1 hare (young)

4 rashers of bacon

2 tablespoons of butter

60g (2oz) of flour

500mls of mixed meat stock

3 onions

1 bay leaf

A teaspoon of peppercorns

2 glasses of port

What you will need to do:

Joint the hare and cut the bacon into strips. Chop and dice the onions.

Melt the butter in a frying pan and brown the hare and fry off the bacon. Put into an oven proof dish. Add the stock and stir in the flour, the peppercorns and the bay leaf.

Cover tightly and cook in a slow (low) oven for 3 hours. After 3 hours, stir in the port. Keep the lid off and continue in the oven until the sauce thickens.

Tighnabruaich Rabbit Stew

SERVES 4

<u>Preparation:</u> wash the rabbit and soak overnight in slightly salted water.

<u>What you will need:</u>

1 rabbit

30g (1oz) of flour

500mls of mixed meat stock

2 onions

3 carrots

Salt and pepper

1 tablespoon of butter

<u>What you will need to do:</u>

Joint the rabbit

Cut and dice the onions and carrots

Season the flour with salt and pepper and coat the joints of rabbit.

Coat the rabbit with the flour and fry in the butter with the carrots and the onions until browned.

Place in a stew pot, cover with the stock and bring to a slow boil. Simmer until tender.

Scots Rabbit Curry

SERVES 6

What you will need:

750mls of mixed meat stock

2 rabbits

6 slices of streaky bacon

4 onions

4 cloves of garlic

A teaspoon of grated ginger

A tablespoon of grated coconut

A teaspoon of cumin

A teaspoon of ground coriander

Half a teaspoon of dried chili powder

Half a teaspoon of turmeric

A quarter of a teaspoon of cayenne pepper

A tablespoon of flour

Half a cup of cream

2 tablespoons of butter

A teaspoon of lemon juice

<u>What you will need to do</u>:

Chop the rabbits up into pieces, chop and dice the onions and chop the garlic and add to the butter in a pan. Brown in the butter and add the stock with the flour, the coconut, ginger, cumin, coriander, cayenne, turmeric and chili.

Cut the bacon up and add to the pot, cover and simmer for half an hour then add the cream and simmer for a further 10 minutes.

Stovies with Lorne

SERVES 4-6

<u>What you will need</u>:

900g (2lbs) of potatoes

6 sliced Lorne sausage

6 onions

Salt and pepper

Tablespoon of butter

Half a cup of water

<u>What you will need to do</u>:

Peel and cube the potatoes and cut and dice the onion. Cut the Lorne sausage into cubes.

Gently fry in the butter for 2 minutes and then add to a non-stick pot with the half a cup of water seasoned with the salt and pepper.

Cover very tightly and simmer on a very gentle heat for 1 hour. Try not to stir too much so as not to break up the potatoes and be very careful with the heat so that it doesn't burn or stick to the bottom of the pan.

Minced Beef Collops

SERVES 6

What you will need:

450g (1lb) of minced beef steak

1 tablespoon of butter

2 onions

250mls of rich beef stock

Tablespoon of oatmeal

What you will need to do:

Melt the butter in a pan

Chop and dice the onions and fry in the butter for 2 minutes then add the minced steak and mix well to prevent the mince from forming lumps.

Add the stock, cover and simmer for 1 hour. Add the oatmeal and cook for another 2 minutes.

Auld Reekie Steak

SERVES 4

<u>What you will need</u>:

4 fillet steaks

1 cup of cream

4 tablespoons of Scotch whisky

125g of grated smoked cheese

25g of butter

Salt and pepper

<u>What you will need to do</u>:

Fry the steaks to your liking

Meantime flambé the whisky then add the cheese and the cream. Simmer gently until reduced by half. Stir in the butter and season with the salt and pepper. Pour over the steaks.

Potted Hough

SERVES 6-8

<u>What you will need</u>:

1200g (3lbs) of beef hough (shin)

1 beef knee or knuckle bone

Salt and plenty of black pepper

<u>What you will need to do</u>:

Remove the fat from the hough (shin) and cube

Put the beef and the bone in a stew pot, cover with water and season with salt and pepper

Bring to a gentle boil and then simmer for 6 hours

Remove bone and meat, discard the bone and finely break up the meat with a fork. Return it to the pot and ensure it is covered by the water it was cooked in – adding more water if required...

Return to the boil and simmer for a further 10 minutes.

Leave it to cool and then press into a mould or a deep dish. Put in the fridge and served sliced, cold.

Stuffed Lamb Shoulder

SERVES 4- 6

<u>What you will need</u>:

1 boned and butterflied shoulder of mutton

200g of your basic breadcrumb stuffing

Sauce (the sauce for venison version one goes very well with this dish)

<u>What you will need to do</u>:

Lay the shoulder flat, skin side down and spread the stuffing over it. Roll as tight as you can and tie with string. Put in a roasting tin and into a pre heated moderate oven for 15 minutes per kg

Lamb Chops with Marmalade

SERVES 4

What you will need:

4 leg of lamb chops

75mls of vinegar

75mls of mixed meat stock

4 tablespoons of marmalade

60g of butter

Salt and pepper

What you will need to do:

Fry to brown the chops in the butter

Season with salt and pepper. Add the vinegar and the stock. Put a tablespoon of marmalade on top of each chop and cover tightly with a lid and simmer gently for 45 minutes.

Pork and Cream

SERVES 4

What you will need:

1 pork filet

1 cup of cream

1 tablespoon of butter

2 cloves of garlic

6 chestnut mushrooms

Salt and pepper

1 teaspoon of wholegrain mustard

What you will need to do:

Cut the fillet into medallions and brown in a pan with the butter.

Chop the mushrooms and the garlic and add to the pan. Toss and gently fry for a minute. Add the cream and the salt and pepper.

Simmer gently uncovered until the cream reduces then stir in the mustard and simmer for a further minute.

Beef Olives

WHAT YOU WILL NEED:

8 beef link sausages (or you can use Lorne sausage-meat)

8 slices of beef (topside)

500mls of mixed meat stock

2 carrots

2 onions

1 clove of garlic

2 tablespoons of oatmeal

1 tablespoon of butter

What you need to do:

Flatten each slice of steak until it is about 1cm thick and then roll it around the sausage (or the sausage-meat made into the shape of a link) and secure with string or cocktail sticks.

Finely chop the onions and garlic and dice the carrots. Fry off in one tablespoon of the butter then add to a large pot.

Brown the beef olives in the remaining butter and then add to the pot. Pour over the stock, cover and simmer for one hour. Stir in the oatmeal to thicken.

STEWS

VEGETABLE STEWS

Vegetable Hotch Potch

SERVES 6-8

What you will need:

1 litres of vegetable stock

6 carrots

6 small white turnips

1 cup (128g) of dried peas

1 cup (128g) of broad beans

Small cauliflower

1 little gem lettuce

6 spring onions

Half a cup (65g) of curly leaf parsley

What you need to do:

Skin **half** of the peas and all of the broad beans and then put half of the peas to one side

Bring stock to the boil and add the skinned peas and broad beans

Peel, cut and dice the carrots and the turnips and add to the pot then simmer for 40 minutes

Meantime cut the cauliflower into florets and chop the lettuce. Cut the spring onions into small pieces. Chop the curly leaf parsley. After the initial 40 minutes simmer, add the remaining half cup of peas, the cauliflower, lettuce and spring onions to the pot. Stir and then add the chopped parsley. This is a thick soup, but you can add more stock if you prefer it a little thinner.

Spicy Green Vegetable Stew

SERVES 6-8

What you will need:

1 litre of vegetable stock

200 grams of green beans

200 grams of broad beans

Half a cup of frozen green peas

200 grams of broccoli

2 stalks of celery

Half a teaspoon of smoked paprika

Half a teaspoon of cumin

Half a teaspoon of chopped ginger

A quarter of a teaspoon of chili powder

Half a cup of green lentils

Knob of butter

What you need to do:

De-shell the broad beans. Remove the fibrous, stringy bits from the celery and finely chop. Wash and chop the green beans and wash and cut the broccoli into florets

Fry off the celery with the butter

Add the broad beans, green beans, peas and lentils to the stock and bring to a gentle simmer and add the celery and the spices. Simmer for 30 minutes

White Bean Stew

SERVES 6-8

<u>What you will need:</u>

1 litre of vegetable stock

400g of haricot beans

400g of chick peas

1 onion

2 sticks of celery

2 carrots

Half a cup of parsley

2 cloves of garlic

Knob of butter

<u>What you need to do:</u>

Chop the onions. Remove the fibrous, stringy bits from the celery. Finely dice the carrots and chop the garlic. Fry the onions, garlic and the celery in the butter until soft.

Add the haricot beans and chick peas to the stock and bring to a gentle simmer then add the onions, garlic and celery.

Chop the parsley and add to the pot and simmer for a further minute.

Spicy Cauliflower and Potato Stew

SERVES 6-8

What you will need:

1 litre of vegetable stock

1 large cauliflower

3 large potatoes

1 onion

2 stalks of celery

Half a teaspoon of smoked paprika

Half a teaspoon of cumin

Half a teaspoon of chopped ginger

A quarter of a teaspoon of chili powder

1 cup of cream

Knob of butter

What you need to do:

Dice the onion. Remove the fibrous, stringy bits from the celery and chop. Peel and dice the potatoes and cut the cauliflower into florets.

Fry off the onion and celery in the butter for a couple of minutes and add to the stock in a pot then add the potatoes, cauliflower and spices. Gently simmer for 20 minutes and then stir in the cream and simmer for a further minute

Barley and Root Vegetable Stew

SERVES 6-8

What you will need:

1.5 litres of vegetable stock

3 large potatoes

Half a swede

3 large carrots

1 parsnip

1 cup of pearl barley

Half a cup of parsley

What you need to do:

Pre-soak the barley overnight in cold water, rinse and add to the stock. Bring to a simmer and simmer for 15 minutes.

Peel and dice the potatoes, carrots, swede and parsnip and add to the pot. Simmer for a further 20 minutes

Finely chop the parsley and add to the post before serving

Quick and Easy Chili Bean and Tomato Stew

SERVES 4-6

What you will need:

Half a litre of vegetable stock

4 large tomatoes

1 tin of chick peas

1 tin of kidney beans

1 onion

One teaspoon of chilli powder (or to preference)

Half a teaspoon of celery salt

Half a teaspoon of garlic salt

Teaspoon of vegetable oil

What you need to do:

Blanche and skin the tomatoes and quarter

Chop the onion and fry off in vegetable oil with the chilli

Add the tomatoes, chick peas, kidney beans and onions to the stock and simmer for 10 minutes

Mixed Lentil and Root Vegetable Stew

SERVES 6-8

<u>What you will need:</u>

1.5 litres of vegetable stock

Half a cup of red lentils

A third of a cup of pay lentils

3 potatoes

Half of a swede

2 large carrots

1 parsnip

<u>What you need to do:</u>

Rinse and add the lentils to half of the stock and bring to a rolling simmer. Simmer for 10 minutes, stirring a few times.

Peel and cut into chunks the potatoes, swede and parsnip

Add the remaining stock to the pot alongside the vegetables, stir and simmer for a further 20 minutes

Barley and Root Vegetable Stew

SERVES 6-8

What you will need:

1 litre of vegetable stock

3 large potatoes

Half a swede

3 large carrots

1 parsnip

1 cup of pearl barley

Half a cup of parsley

What you need to do:

Pre-soak the barley overnight, add to the stock and simmer for 15 minutes

Peel, chop and dice the potatoes, swede, carrots and parsnip and add to the pot along with the remaining stock

Simmer for a further 20 minutes

Finely chop the parsley and add just before serving

CHICKEN STEWS

Basic Chicken Stew

SERVES 6-8

<u>What you will need:</u>

2 cups of chicken stock

1 cup of dry white wine

8 chicken thigh fillets

2 tablespoons butter

2 large onions

3 carrots

2 sprigs thyme

4 potatoes

1 cup of parsley

<u>What you will need to do:</u>

Fry the chicken in the butter until browned

Peel and finely dice the onions, carrots and potatoes and add to the pot. Add the sprigs of thyme, mix thoroughly and then add the chicken stock. Cover and simmer for 40 minutes, remove the thyme and add the white wine.

Finely chop the parsley, add to the pot, mix and simmer for a further 5 minutes. Thicken with flour or corn flour (corn starch)

Chicken, Mushroom and Port Stew

SERVES 4-6

<u>What you will need:</u>

1 whole chicken

Half a litre of chicken stock

1 cup of port

200g of mushrooms

2 tablespoons butter

<u>What you will need to do:</u>

Joint the chicken and brown in the butter

Chop the mushrooms and add to the pot and continue frying for a few minutes then add the stock.

Cover and simmer for 40 minutes then add the port.

Simmer for a further 10 minutes. Thicken with flour or corn flour (corn starch)

Chicken, Chicken Liver and Onion Stew

SERVES 4

What you will need:

Half a litre of chicken stock

4 skinned chicken thighs

150g of chicken livers

2 onions

1 stick of celery

Knob of butter

What you will need to do:

Peel and dice the onions. Remove the fibrous, stringy bits from the celery and finely chop and then fry until soft in the butter. Chop the chicken livers and add to the pot and fry for a minute

Add the chicken thighs and the stock, cover and simmer for 40 minutes. Thicken with flour or corn flour (corn starch)

Chicken and Butterbean Stew

SERVES 4

What you will need:

2 cups of chicken stock

1 large tin of butterbeans

4 skinned chicken thighs

2 stalks of celery

4 shallots

1 teaspoon of paprika

2 tablespoons of tomato puree

Knob of butter

What you will need to do:

peel and chop the shallots. Remove the fibrous stringy bits from the celery and chop then fry off in the butter and the paprika with the onions for a few minutes then add the tomato puree

add the chicken thighs and cover with the stock and simmer for 40 minutes

Add the butterbeans and simmer for a further 5 minutes

Spicy Chicken and Tomato Stew

SERVES 4

What you will need:

2 cups of chicken stock

4 chicken thighs

6 tomatoes

1 tablespoon of tomato puree

Half a teaspoon of cumin

Half a teaspoon of smoked paprika

Half a teaspoon of chilli powder

4 skinned chicken thighs

2 stalks of celery

2 onions

Knob of butter

What you will need to do:

Peel and chop the onions. Remove the fibrous stringy bits from the celery and chop. Fry the onions and the celery in the butter with the spices for a few minutes Add the stock, the tomato puree and the chicken thighs, cover and simmer for 40 minutes

Blanche and quarter the tomatoes and add to the pot with the tomato puree and simmer for a further 10 minutes

BEEF STEWS

Stew and Dook

SERVES 6-8

This stew is **not** served browned nor thickened.

<u>What you will need</u>:

1 litre of rich beef stock

1200g (3lbs) beef Hough (shin)

250g of minced beef

3 beef kidneys

6 onions

<u>What you will need to do</u>:

Remove the fat from the Hough (shin) and cube

Chop and dice the onions

Cut the kidneys length ways and remove as much of the fat gristle from the middle. Chop.

Bring the stock to a gentle boil and add the cubed Hough, the minced beef, the diced onions and the kidneys.

Simmer very gently for 3 hours and add additional salt and black pepper if required

Serve in a bowl and then dook (dip) in your bread

Beef and Pickled Walnut Stew

SERVES 4-6

What you will need:

500mls of rich beef stock

500g of shin

200g of pickled walnuts

200mls of port

Handful of parsley

2 onions

1 tablespoon of flour

2 knobs of butter of butter

What you will need to do:

Chop and dice the onions. Cut the walnuts in half

Cube the shin dip in the flour and then brown in a pan with one knob of butter. When brown add to the stock, cover and simmer for 2 hours.

Fry the onions with the second knob of butter until browned and soft and then add to the stock with the pickled walnuts and the port and simmer for a further 30 minutes

Chop the parsley and add to the pot before serving

Thicken with flour or corn flour (corn starch)

Oxtail Stew

SERVES 4

What you will need:

500mls of rich beef stock

1 whole ox tail

2 carrots

2 onions

1 tablespoon of flour

1 tablespoon of butter

What you will need to do:

Chop and dice the carrots and onions.

Remove excess fa and cut the ox tail into joints. Dip in the flour and brown in a pan with the butter. When brown add to the stock, cover and simmer for 2 hours then add the vegetables and simmer for a further 30 minutes.

Thicken with flour or corn flour (corn starch)

Everyday Beef Stew

SERVES 6-8

What you will need:

500mls of rich beef stock

1kg of beef shin

4 carrots

3 onions

2 parsnips

6 small white turnips

1 tablespoon of flour

I tablespoon of butter

What you will need to do:

Chop and dice the carrots, parsnips, turnips and onions

Cube the shin and dip in the flour and brown in a pan with the butter. When brown add the stock and simmer for 2 hours.

After 2 hours, add the vegetables and cover and simmer for a further 30 minutes

Thicken with flour or corn flour (corn starch)

Beef Stew with Potatoes and Swede

SERVES 4

<u>What you will need</u>:

500mls of rich beef stock

500g of beef shin

1 small swede (approx. 500g)

2 onions

1 stick of celery

4 large potatoes

200mls of red wine

1 tablespoon of flour

Knob of butter

<u>What you will need to do</u>:

Remove the fibrous, stringy bitts from the celery and chop. Peel and dice the swede, potatoes and onions

Dice the beef shin and coat in the flour and fry until browned in the butter and then add to the stock, cover and simmer for 2 hours.

After 2 hours, add the diced vegetables and the wine to the pan and cook for a further 30 minutes

Thicken with flour or corn flour (corn starch)

Spicy Minced Beef Stew

SERVES 4

What you will need:

500mls of rich beef stock

500g of minced beef

2 carrots

2 onions

1 celery stalk

Half a teaspoon of cumin

Half a teaspoon of smoked paprika

Half a teaspoon of chilli powder

2 large tomatoes

1 tablespoon of butter

What you will need to do:

Dice the onions

Brown the minced beef and the diced onions in the butter along with the spices

Remove the fibrous, stringy bits from the celery, chop and add to the mince and onions

Peel and dice the carrots, blanche the tomatoes and roughly chop then add to the pot along with the stock

Cover and simmer for 1 hour

Thicken with flour or corn flour (corn starch)

Beef Stew and Butterbeans

SERVES 8

What you will need:

1 litre of rich beef stock

500g of minced beef

500g of shin

2 onions

400g of butterbeans

Knob of butter

Tablespoon of flour

What you will need to do:

Dice the onions

Dice the shin and coat in the flour. Mix through the minced beef and add the onions then brown off in the butter

Add to the stock, cover and simmer for 2 hours then add a 400g tin of butterbeans and simmer for a further 30 minutes.

Thicken with flour or corn flour (corn starch)

Mixed Bean and Beef Stew

SERVES 8-10

<u>What you will need:</u>

1.5 litres of rich beef stock

500g of minced beef

500g of shin

2 onions

200g of butterbeans

200g of haricot beans

200g chick peas

200g of red kidney beans

Knob of butter

Tablespoon of flour

Flour or cornflour (corn flour) to thicken

<u>What you will need to do:</u>

Dice the onions

Dice the shin and coat in the flour. Mix through the minced beef and add the onions then brown off in the butter

Add to the stock, cover and simmer for 2 hours then add the butterbeans, haricot beans, chick peas and red kidney beans and simmer for a further 30 minutes.

Thicken with the flour or corn flour (corn starch)

Beef and Stout Stew

SERVES 8-10

<u>What you will need</u>:

1 litres of rich beef stock

100g of smoked streaky bacon

2 cans of stout

1kg of shin

3 onions

2 knobs of butter

Tablespoon of flour

Flour or cornflour (corn flour) to thicken

<u>What you will need to do</u>:

Dice the shin, roll in the flour and brown in a pan with one nob of the butter. Add to the beef stock, cover and simmer for 2 hours

Dice the onions and finely chop the bacon and fry with the second knob of butter until onions are soft. Add to the stock with the stout and simmer for a further 30 minutes.

Thicken with the flour or corn flour (corn starch)

LAMB STEWS

Pan Cooked Gigot and Barley Stew

SERVES 6

What you will need:

1 gigot (leg) of mutton

4 carrots

6 white turnips

2 onions

1 litre of your vegetable, brisket and lamb stock

Half a cup of pearl barley

What you will need to do:

Get your butcher to cut the gigot into slices (chops)

Put the chops in a large stew pot and add the stock. Bring to the boil and skim. Simmer gently for 1 hour then add the barley and simmer for a further half an hour.

Chop and dice the carrots, turnip and onions and add to the pot. Simmer for a further hour.

Thicken with flour or corn flour (corn starch)

Lamb and Root Vegetable Stew

SERVES 10-12

What you will need:

1 shoulder of lamb

1.5 litres of lamb and vegetable stock

6 potatoes

1 small swede

2 parsnips

6 carrots

6 small white turnips

8 shallots

2 stalks of celery

Half a cup of green lentils

2 knobs of butter

What you will need to do:

Trim the excess fat from the shoulder of lamb and roast the shoulder of lamb in a hot oven for 30 minutes then remove from the oven and add to the stock. Cover and simmer for two and a half hours Chop and dice all of the vegetables (remembering to remove the fibrous, stringy bits from the celery) and fry in a large pan with the butter.

Add to the stock after it has simmered for the two and a half hours then rinse and add the lentils and simmer for a further hour. Remove the lamb, 'pull' apart with a fork and add back into the stock

Lamb and Cauliflower Stew

SERVES 4-6

What you will need:

500g of lamb shoulder

500mls of lamb and vegetable stock

1 whole small cauliflower (or half of a large cauliflower)

2 onions

2 stalks of celery

4 tomatoes

Tablespoon of flour

2 knobs of butter

What you will need to do:

Remove the excess fat from the lamb and cut into cubes then dust with the flour and brown in a pan with one knob of the butter. Add to the stock, cover and simmer for 2 and a half hours

Dice the onions. Remove the fibrous, stringy bits from the celery and chop then fry off the onions and the celery with the second knob of butter until soft

Blanch, skin and chop the tomatoes. Cut the cauliflower into florets

After the 2 and half hours simmering time, add the onions, celery, tomatoes and cauliflower florets and simmer for a further 30 minutes

Thicken if required with flour or corn flour (corn starch)

Lamb and chickpea Stew

SERVES 4-6

<u>What you will need</u>:

500g of lamb shoulder

500mls of lamb and vegetable stock

1 large can of chickpeas

2 stalks of celery

2 onions

1 teaspoon of smoked paprika

2 sprigs of rosemary

1 tablespoon of flour

1 knob of butter

<u>What you will need to do</u>:

Dice the onions and cut up the celery (removing the fibrous stringy bits)

Remove the excess fat from the lamb and cut into cubes. Dust with flour and brown in a pan then add the diced onions and the celery along with the paprika and mix through thoroughly

Add the sprig of rosemary then pour over the stock, cover and simmer for 3 hours

Add the drained tin of chickpeas and simmer for a further 10 minutes. Remove the sprig of rosemary before serving

Lamb Stew with Mint and Peas

SERVES 4-6

What you will need:

500g of lamb shoulder

500mls of lamb and vegetable stock

3 cups of frozen garden peas

2 stalks of celery

2 onions

2 tablespoons of fresh mint

2 sprigs of rosemary

1 tablespoon of flour

1 knob of butter

2 tablespoons of chopped parsley

What you will need to do:

Dice the onions and cut up the celery (removing the fibrous stringy bits)

Remove the excess fat from the lamb and cut into cubes. Dust with flour and brown in a pan then add the diced onions and the celery and mix through thoroughly

Add the sprig of rosemary then pour over the stock, cover and simmer for 3 hours

Add the frozen peas and simmer for a further 10 minutes. Finely chop and then add the fresh mint. Remove the sprig of rosemary before serving

Pearl Barley Lamb Shanks (oven cooked)

SERVES 4-6

<u>What you will need</u>:

4 lamb shanks

500mls of lamb and vegetable stock

Half a cup of pearl barley

2 onions

1 sprig of rosemary

2 knobs of butter

<u>What you will need to do</u>:

Pre-soak the pearl barley overnight in cold water

Prepare your shanks by removing the outer fibrous skin and then brown in a pan with one of the knobs of butter

Dice the onions and gently soften in a pan with the other knob of butter

Add the shanks and the onions to the stock in a large ovenproof dish then stir in the barley and throw in the rosemary

Cover and cook in the oven on a medium heat for 3 hours

Thicken with flour or cornflour (corn starch)

Remove the rosemary before serving

Spiced lamb Stew

SERVES 4-6

<u>What you will need</u>:

500g of lamb shoulder

500mls of lamb and vegetable stock

6 tomatoes

1 tablespoon of tomato puree

Half a teaspoon of cumin

Half a teaspoon of smoked paprika

Half a teaspoon of chilli powder

2 stalks of celery

2 onions

Knob of butter

<u>What you will need to do</u>:

Dice the onions

Remove the excess fat from the lamb and cut into cubes. Dust with flour and brown in a pan then add the diced onions in the along with the spices and mix through thoroughly

Remove the fibrous, stringy bits from the celery, chop and add to the pan Peel and dice the carrots, blanche and skin the tomatoes and roughly chop then add to the pot along with the stock and the tomato puree

Cover and simmer for 3 hours Thicken with flour or corn flour (corn starch)

GAME STEWS

Game Fowl Stew

SERVES 8

What you will need:

1 litre of chicken stock

1 partridge

1 small chicken

1 grouse

1 partridge

2 leeks

500g of potatoes

2 carrots

2 sticks of celery

Half a cup of flour

What you will need to do:

Joint all of the birds, dust with flour and fry until golden brown

Chop and dice the potatoes and carrots. Cut the celery into small pieces (having removed the fibrous stringy bits). Cut up the leeks into small pieces. Add the jointed birds and the vegetables to the stock, bring to the boil and then gently simmer for 25 minutes.

Pheasant stew

SERVES 4

What you will need:

250mls of chicken stock

1 pheasant

1 tablespoon of flour

1 tablespoon of butter

A half a glass of claret

3 rashers of bacon

Salt and pepper

A tablespoon of chopped flat leaf parsley

What you will need to do:

Joint the bird and dust with flour and fry in the butter until golden brown. Put into a stew pot with the stock and claret. Chop and dice the bacon then add to the pot. Cover and gently simmer for 1 hour.

Garnish with the parsley.

Pheasant stew with cider and bacon (made as a casserole in the oven)

SERVES 6

What you will need:

300mls of chicken stock

2 pheasants

100g of bacon

2 apples

2 sticks of celery

Tablespoon of butter

4 sage leaves

500mls of cider

1 savoy cabbage

100mls of cream

What you will need to do:

Pre-heat the oven to 170 degrees C

Melt the butter in a frying pan, season the birds and brown in the pan. Put the birds in an ovenproof dish. Chop the bacon and dice the onion. Cut up the celery (after removing the fibrous stringy bits) and cut up the sage. Add all of these ingredients to the pan and fry gently for 10 minutes, remove excess fat. Cut up the apples and place over the pheasants. Chop the cabbage and add to the dish with the stock and the cider. Cover and put in the oven for 25 minutes then mix the cream through the dish.

Hare Casserole

SERVES 4

<u>What you will need</u>:

1 hare (young)

4 rashers of bacon

2 tablespoons of butter

60g (2oz) of flour

500mls of mixed meat stock

3 onions

1 bay leaf

A teaspoon of peppercorns

2 glasses of port

<u>What you will need to do</u>:

Joint the hare and cut the bacon into strips. Chop and dice the onions.

Melt the butter in a frying pan and brown the hare and fry off the bacon. Put into an oven proof dish. Add the stock and stir in the flour, the peppercorns and the bay leaf.

Cover tightly and cook in a slow (low) oven for 3 hours. After 3 hours, stir in the port. Keep the lid off and continue in the oven until the sauce thickens.

Tighnabruaich Rabbit Stew

SERVES 4

What you will need:

1 rabbit

30g (1oz) of flour

500mls of mixed meat stock

2 onions

3 carrots

Salt and pepper

1 tablespoon of butter

What you will need to do:

Joint the rabbit

Cut and dice the onions and carrots

Season the flour with salt and pepper and coat the joints of rabbit. and fry in the butter with the carrots and the onions until browned.

Place in a stew pot, cover with the stock and bring to a slow boil. Simmer until tender.

Venison Stew

SERVES 4

<u>What you will need</u>:

Half a litre of mixed meat stock

500g of venison shoulder

Knob of butter

2 parsnips

4 potatoes

3 onions

2 cloves of garlic

1 bay leaf

1 teaspoon of celery salt

Tablespoon of flour

<u>What you will need to do</u>:

Cube the venison and dust with the flour then brown in the butter. Add to the stock, cover and simmer for one and a half hours

Peel and chop the parsnips and the onions and mince the garlic

Peel and cube the potatoes and then add all of the vegetables with the celery salt and the bay leaf to the pot and cook for a further 20 minutes

Remove the bay leaf and thicken if required with flour

FISH STEWS

Creamy Tomato Fish Stew

SERVES 4

<u>What you will need</u>:

1 cup of basic fish stock

200g of cod fillet

200g of haddock (or whiting) fillet

4 tomatoes

Half a teaspoon of celery salt

1 cup of cream

<u>What you will need to do</u>:

Blanche, skin and chop the tomatoes and put in a pan with the stock. Add the celery salt and, uncovered, simmer for 10 minutes and then add the cream (stir, ensuring the cream doesn't split) and simmer uncovered for a further 5 minutes

Skin and cube the fish and add to the pot. Simmer for a further 5 minutes

Whiting Stew with Leeks and Bacon

SERVES 4

What you will need:

1 cup of basic fish stock

8 whiting fillets

1 large leek

1 stalk of celery

2 rashers of lean smoky bacon

1 potato

1 carrot

1 tablespoon of parsley

1 knob of butter

1 teaspoon of vegetable oil

What you will need to do:

Peel and cube the potato and cook in the fish stock until soft then mash to thicken the stock

Wash and finely chop the leek. Remove the fibrous, stringy bits from the celery and finely chop. Dice the lean bacon and fry until crispy in the vegetable oil. Meantime, fry off the leeks and celery in the butter until soft. Add the bacon, leeks and celery to the potato and stock and bring back to a gentle simmer (add more stock if required)

Add the fish and simmer for 10 minutes. Chop the parsley and add just before serving

Luxury Fish Stew

SERVES 6

<u>What you will need</u>:

1 cup of the rich shellfish stock

1 cup of cream

200g of skinned cod fillet

200g of skinned haddock (or whiting) fillet

200g of prawns

1 lobster tail

2 skinned salmon fillets

1 onion

1 clove of garlic

1 bulb of fennel

1 knob of butter

2 tablespoons of chopped coriander

<u>What you will need to do</u>:

Dice the onion, crush the garlic and finely slice the fennel and fry until soft with the knob of butter.

Skin and cube the white fish. Cut the lobster tail into 6 pieces, Cut each salmon fillet into 3 pieces.

Bring your stock to a gentle simmer and add the onions and fennel.

Add the lobster tail. Simmer for 1 minute and then add the cubed white fish and the salmon. Simmer for a further minute and then add the prawns and the cream and simmer for 2 minutes. Thicken with flour or cornflour (corn starch) if required and add the chopped coriander before serving

Spicy Fish Stew

SERVES 4

What you will need:

4 skinned salmon fillets

200g of prawns

1 cup of basic fish stock

2 cloves of garlic

1 onion

200g of red kidney beans

4 tomatoes

1 potato

Half a teaspoon of chilli powder

Half a teaspoon of turmeric

Half a teaspoon of ground ginger

Half a teaspoon of cumin

Half a cup of cream

A tablespoon of chopped coriander

Knob of butter

What you will need to do:

Peel and finely dice the potatoes. Dice the onion and slice the garlic and add everything to a pan with the butter and fry until soft. Add the spices and mix through thoroughly

Blanche, skin and chop the tomatoes and add to the stock along with the spiced potatoes, onions and garlic. Simmer for 10 minutes and then add the kidney beans and the fish

Simmer for a further 5 minutes and then stir in the cream. Simmer for a further 5 minutes

Add the coriander just before serving

Fish Stew with Garlic and Butterbeans

SERVES 4

What you will need:

1 cup of basic fish stock

1 onion

200g of skinned cod fillets

200g of skinned haddock (or whiting fillets)

1 large can (400g) of butterbeans

1 whole garlic bulb

2 stalks of celery

Half a cup of frozen garden peas

Teaspoon of vegetable oil

Knob of butter

1 teaspoon of dill

What you will need to do:

Rub the vegetable oil into the bulb of garlic, wrap in tinfoil and roast for 30 minutes in a hot oven.

Dice the onions and chop the celery and fry until soft in the butter

When the garlic has roasted sufficiently to allow you to squeeze it out of the cloves, add the garlic to the onions and celery and then mix through the frozen peas. Add this mixture to the fish stock and simmer for 10 minutes

Cube the fish and add to the pan and simmer for a further 5 minutes then add the butterbeans and continue simmering for a further 5 minutes

Add the dill just before serving

BRIDIES AND SAVOURY PIES

Different pastry is used for different bridies and pies. Short crust pastry, hot water pastry and puff pastry are used.

Short crust pastry – 225g of plain flour, 100g of butter, pinch of salt, 3 tablespoons of water.

Cut the butter into cubes. Sift the flour into a bowl and rub in the butter until the mixture resembles fine breadcrumbs. Mix in the salt and the water and knead slightly and wrap in cling film. Put in the fridge to cool.

Hot water pastry – 500g of plain flour, 175g of lard, 225g of water, pinch of salt and a little milk for glazing.

Sift the flour and the salt into a bowl. Heat the lard in the water and put it into a well you create in the flour. Mix thoroughly.

Rough puff pastry – 250g of strong plain flour and 250g of butter. Pinch of salt. 3 tablespoons of water.

Cut the butter into cubes. Sift the flour into a bowl. Add the salt and the cubed butter. Using your fingertips, rub in the butter slightly but do not go as far as breadcrumbs. The butter should remain visible in the mix. Make a well in the mix and add the water. Mix and form a ball. Put in cling film and put in the fridge.

When you roll out the dough ensure you don't work the butter too much. Roll it until the pastry is 3 times the original width.

Minced Beef Collops Round

SERVES 4

<u>What you will need</u>:

Short crust pastry

Rough puff pastry

Cooked minced beef collops

Milk for glazing

<u>What you need to do</u>:

Roll out the short crust pastry and line a greased 22cm round pie tin. Pierce the pastry with a fork and blind bake until cooked.

Add the cooked minced collops mix.

Rollout the rough puff pastry and top the pie. Score and glaze with the milk. Bake in a pre-heated hot oven. Turn the pie around in the oven after 10 minutes and cook for another 5 minutes.

Forfar Bridies

SERVES 3

What you will need:

900g of short crust pastry

900g of topside steak

Half a cup of shredded suet

1 onion

Salt and pepper

Milk for glazing

What you will need to do:

Cut and dice the steak into small pieces and season with the salt and pepper.

Chop and dice the onion and add it to the steak.

Divide the pastry into 3, roll out thinly into an oval shape. Cover half the pastry with the steak and onion and top with shredded suet.

Fold and using water, crimp around the edges. Slice a hole in the top and glaze with milk.

Bake in a hot oven for 30 minutes.

Venison Bridies

Serves 3

Make as for Forfar bridies, replacing the steak with breast of venison cut small and adding 100mls of rich beef stock to moisten the meat.

Scottish Mutton Pies

SERVES 3

What you will need:

900g of hot water pastry

900g of lean mutton

1 onion

250mls of the vegetable, brisket and lamb stock

2 teaspoons of cornflour

Milk to glaze

What you will need to do:

Knead the pastry on a floured board until smooth. Remove a quarter of the pastry to keep for the lids. Cut the pastry into 3 pieces and mould it around the bottom of a glass to shape.

Chop and dice the onion. Cut the mutton into small pieces and mix with the onion. Use a little of the stock to moisten and share the mixture between the 6 pastry cases. Use the remaining pastry for 6 lids. Cover each of the pies with lids, wetting the edges and cut a hole in the top.

Glaze with the milk and bake in a moderate oven for 40 minutes.

Meantime mix the cornflour with a little of the stock. Bring the remaining stock to a boil and stir in enough of the cornflour to thicken.

When the pies are done, pour a little of the gravy in through the hole on top of the pies.

Kingdom of Fife Pie

SERVES 6

What you will need:

900g of rough puff pastry

1 rabbit

900g of pickled pork

100mls of rich beef stock

Half a cup of liver stuffing

A half a teaspoon of nutmeg

2 tablespoons of white wine

Milk for glazing

What you will need to do:

Cut the rabbit into 6 pieces and soak in cold water for an hour.

Cut and dice the pickled pork and season with salt, pepper and the nutmeg.

Mix the liver stuffing with the stock to make a gravy. Put the rabbit, the pork and the gravy into a pie dish and cover with thinly rolled rough puff pastry.

Cut holes in the pastry for ventilation and bake in a moderate oven for one and a half hours.

Scottish Steak and Kidney Pie

SERVES 6

What you will need:

2 cups of rich beef stock

900g of rough puff pastry

900g of lean stewing steak (shin is best)

450g of ox kidneys

6 beef link sausages (the seasoning in the sausages helps to season the pie filling)

Tablespoon of flour

Milk for glazing

What you will need to do:

Trim and dice the stewing steak and cut each beef link into 3 pieces. Cut the kidneys length ways and remove the gristle in the middle. Toss these ingredients in the flour and add to the stock. Bring to a gentle boil and gently simmer for 45 minutes then put in a large pie dish.

Rollout your pastry thinly and cover the pie filling, crimping the edges. Score with a knife and glaze with milk.

Bake in a moderate oven for 45 minutes or until the pastry is fully cooked.

Macaroni and Cheese Pie

SERVES 4

What you will need:

900g of hot water pastry

350g of macaroni pasta

100mls of milk

300g of grated cheese

Teaspoon of mustard

Teaspoon of salt

Black pepper

What you will need to do:

Cook the macaroni in salted water and drain. Mix through the milk and 250g of the grated cheese. Season with black pepper. Add the mustard. Leave to stand for 5 minutes whilst the pasta absorbs the cheesy milk.

Prepare 4 pastry shells (as for mutton pies) but use all the pastry as these pies do not have lids. Bake the shells in a moderate oven until cooked through.

Fill the 4 pie shells with the macaroni and cheese. Sprinkle the remaining cheese on top and put back in the oven for 5 minutes.

Serve immediately.

A Bride's Pie

SERVES 4

What you will need:

900g of rough puff pastry

The meat of 2 previously boiled calves' feet

450g of mutton suet

450g of sliced apples

200g of currants

200g of raisins

Half a teaspoon of ground cinnamon

Half a teaspoon of grated nutmeg

A teaspoon of candied orange peel

A teaspoon of lemon peel

1 glass of brandy

1 glass of Madeira

What you will need to do:

Mix the chopped calves feet meat, the suet and the apples and add the fruit, the cinnamon, nutmeg and orange and lemon peel. Mix in the brandy and the Madeira.

Line a loose bottomed pie tin with pastry and cover with the mixture. Roll out the remaining pastry and cover. Cut a hole for ventilation.

Bake in a hot oven for 45 minutes or until the pastry is cooked.

(Traditionally, a gold wedding ring was placed under the pastry lid and the top was decorated with cupids.)

Scots Potato 'Pie'

SERVES 6

What you will need:

6 medium to large potatoes of roughly the same size

Cooked scraps of meat (whatever you have in the fridge)

1 onion

2 tablespoons of butter

1 teaspoon of cornflour

1 cup of basic vegetable stock

Salt and pepper.

What you will need to do:

Carefully peel the potatoes

Cut off a 3mm (half an inch) slice from the top of each potato and keep as lids.

Hollow out the centre of each of the potatoes leaving the potato 13mm thick all over.

Finely chop or mince your scraps of meat and finely dice your scooped-out potato.

Part boil the onion and mix through the minced scraps of meats and your diced potato. Season with salt and pepper.

Add the cornflour to the stock and bring to a slow boil. When thickened add a little to your mix to moisten.

Stuff the potatoes with this mixture, put on the potato lids and brush all over with melted butter. Place in a well-greased baking tin. Bake in a moderate oven for at least an hour. Baste with more melted butter throughout the cooking period.

BANNOCKS

BANNOCKS CAN BE EITHER leavened (with baking powder or baking soda added) or unleavened (similar to a flatbread). They can be savoury or sweet.

They are a simple, traditional bread originating in Scotland and can be made outside on a fire on a bannock stane (stone), indoors on a griddle. Or in the oven.

It can be griddled dry, baked or fried using flour, barley or oatmeal.

Barley Bannocks

SERVES 4-6

What you will need:

250mls of milk

Pinch of salt

1 tablespoon of butter

Half a cup of barley meal

Tablespoon of flour

What you will need to do:

Bring the milk to the boil with the butter and the pinch of salt. Stir the barley meal in quickly and stir continuously until it makes a dough.

Flour a board and turn out the dough. Roll out thinly and cut into 6 rounds.

Ideally you need a hot girdle, but a large non-stick frying pan will do. Bake on the hot girdle or the hot frying pan, turning once.

Eat hot.

Pitcaithly Bannocks

SERVES 6

What you will need:

115g of butter

A pinch of salt

100g of caster sugar

1 cup of flour

A tablespoon of rice flour

A tablespoon of mixed peel

A tablespoon of flaked almonds

What you will need to do:

Cream the butter and sugar together and mix in the flour and the pinch of salt. Add the mixed peel and the flaked almonds.

Roll out into a cake about 13mm thick. Pinch the edges and place on a greased baking tin.

Bake in a moderate oven for about 30 minutes and cool on a wire tray.

Ardentinny Drop Bannocks

SERVES 6

What you will need:

1 egg

500mls of milk

Half a teaspoon of baking soda

A pinch of salt

3 tablespoons of oatmeal

What you will need to do:

Beat the egg in a large bowl and stir in the milk. Mix in the baking soda and the salt, then mix in the oatmeal and stir until it forms a medium consistency batter.

Lightly grease a pre-heated griddle or heavy frying pan and drop a spoonful of mixture onto the heated pan. Repeat.

You will see the mixture rise and bubble as it cooks. Turn when golden (after about a minute) and brown gently on the other side.

Oat Bannocks (version 1)

SERVES 4

<u>What you will need</u>:

2 tablespoons of butter

1 cup of course oats

A quarter of a cup of whole fat milk

Half a teaspoon of salt

<u>What you will need to do</u>:

Melt the butter in a pan and add the milk

Warm through and add the salt and the oats and mix thoroughly

With floured hands, turn the mixture out onto a floured board and split into 4 equal portions. Flatten and cook on a lightly greased griddle or heavy frying pan for a minute on each side.

Oat Bannocks (version 2)

SERVES 6

<u>What you will need:</u>

1 cup rolled oats

1 cup oat flour

A quarter of a teaspoon salt

6 tablespoons of chilled unsalted butter

Half a cup of milk

1 egg yolk

<u>What you will need to do:</u>

Mix together the oats, oat flour and sugar and break in and mix through the butter.

Add the milk and mix thoroughly until a dough is formed, then on a floured board, roll out the mixture and put on a greased baking tray. Gently mark the top into squares

Brush the egg yolk over the top and bake for 20 minutes in a moderate oven (180 degrees C)

Oat Bannocks (version 3)

SERVES 4

<u>What you will need</u>:

1 and a half cups of cold, cooked porridge oats

1 and a half cups of self-raising flour

A quarter of a teaspoon salt

6 tablespoons of chilled unsalted butter

A quarter of a cup of milk

A teaspoon of baking soda

<u>What you will need to do</u>:

Mix the flour, salt and baking soda with the cooked porridge and mix thoroughly.

Add the milk and form into a sticky dough

Turn out onto a floured board, roll out into a circle and place on a greased baking tray

Mark (don't cut) into 4 equal pieces

Bake in a hot oven (200 degrees C) for 20 minutes

Fried Bannocks

SERVES 4

What you will need:

1 cup plain flour

1 tablespoon of sugar

1 teaspoon of baking powder

A quarter of a teaspoon of salt

A quarter of a cup of cold milk

2 tablespoons of lard (or vegetable oil if preferred)

What you will need to do:

Mix all the ingredients together to form a batter. Oil your hands and split the mixture into 4 balls

Flatten the balls

Heat a deep frying pan and melt the lard

Fry the flattened balls until golden on each side

Fruit Bannocks

ON THE STANE (FOR BAKING on a bannock stone next to a campfire… you can use a heavy baking tray)

Serves 4

What you will need:

1 cup plain flour

1 cup of mixed fruit (sultanas, currants, raisins)

1 tablespoon of sugar

1 teaspoon of baking powder

A quarter of a teaspoon of salt

A quarter of a cup of cold milk

What you will need to do:

Mix the flour, sugar, salt, fruit and baking powder together then stir in the milk. Mix thoroughly into a sticky dough. Pat onto the stone or into the tray and bake, turning once, until cooked through

SCONES
SAVOURY AND SWEET

Potato scones (version 1)

SERVES 4

What you will need:

450g of cold cooked mashed potato

Approximately half a cup of flour

A half a teaspoon of salt

What you will need to do:

Add the salt and the flour to the mashed potatoes and knead into a dough.

Cut into 4 and form into rounds.

Make 4 triangles from each round and brown both sides on a hot girdle or non-stick frying pan.

Special Potato scones (version 2)

SERVES 4

What you will need:

Half a cup of oatmeal

450g of cooked, mashed potatoes

A half teaspoon of salt

2 tablespoons of flour

What you will need to do:

To the mashed potatoes, add the salt and the oatmeal and mix in the flour.

Roll out thinly and cut into triangles.

Cook on a hot girdle or non-stick frying pan, turning once and ensuring they are browned on both sides.

Sour Scones

SERVES 4-6

What you will need:

Pre-soak a cup of oatmeal with a cup of buttermilk, cover and store in the fridge for a few days.

A cup of flour

A teaspoon of sugar

A teaspoon of caraway seeds

What you will need to do:

Mix the flour into the milk and oatmeal, add the sugar and the caraway seeds. Make into a soft dough, roll out and cut into rounds. Bake on the girdle or frying pan. Cook them steadily on the one side for about 5 minutes. You will see them begin to rise. Turn and give them about 5 minutes on the other side.

Cheese scones

SERVES 6

What you will need:

200g of self-raising flour

Half a teaspoon of dry mustard

Half a teaspoon of salt

50g of butter

125g of grated cheese

1 egg

Tablespoon of water

What you will need to do:

Sift the flour, salt and mustard into a bowl. Rub in the butter and add the grated cheese. Use a little of the water and mix. Roll out onto a floured board (one inch thick). Cut into rounds and brush with beaten egg. Bake in a hot oven (200 degrees C) until you see that they have well risen (10 to 15 minutes)

Wholemeal scones

SERVES 8-10

<u>What you will need</u>:

250g of wholemeal flour

250g of self-raising flour

A half teaspoon of salt

400mls milk

50g of butter

1 egg

<u>What you will need to do</u>:

Sift the flour and rub in the butter. Add the salt and mix through with the milk (ensure the mixture is not too wet)

Form into a dough and turn out onto a floured board

Roll to 1 inch thick and cut into 12 - 15 scones.

Brush with the beaten egg and bake at 200 degrees C for approximately 15 minutes

Herb scones

SERVES 8-10

What you will need:

500g of self-raising flour

Half a teaspoon of salt

A shake of pepper

1 teaspoon of mixed herbs

50g of butter

1 egg

200mls of milk

What you will need to do:

Sift the flour, salt and pepper into a bowl. Rub in the butter and add the mixed herbs and the milk. Turn out onto a floured board and roll to one inch thick. Cut into rounds and brush with the beaten egg. Bake at 200 degrees C for approximately 15 minutes.

Sultana scones

SERVES 8-10

What you will need:

500g of self-raising flour

Half a teaspoon of salt

1 tablespoon of caster sugar

1half a cup of sultanas

50g of butter

1 egg

200mls of milk

What you will need to do:

Sift the flour, salt and sugar into a bowl. Rub in the butter and add the sultanas and the milk. Turn out onto a floured board and roll to one inch thick. Cut into rounds and brush with the beaten egg. Bake at 200 degrees C for approximately 15 minutes.

Apple scones

SERVES 8-10

Follow the recipe for sultana scones but replace the sultanas with 1 grated apple

White girdle scones

SERVES 8

What you will need:

450g of flour

A teaspoon of cream of tartar

A half a teaspoon of salt

A cup of buttermilk

What you will need to do:

Sieve the flour into a bowl and add the other ingredients to make a soft dough.

Turn out onto a floured board, roll and cut into 4. Flatten each piece into a round scone and divide these into quarters.

Flour and bake on a hot girdle or non-stick frying pan and turn when they are well risen and going brown on the one side. They should cook for about 5 minutes on both sides.

Treacle scones

SERVES 6-8

<u>What you will need</u>:

1 cup of flour

2 tablespoons of butter

Half a teaspoon of baking soda

Half a teaspoon of cream of tartar

Half a teaspoon of cinnamon

Half a teaspoon of ground ginger

A pinch of salt

1 tablespoon of treacle

Half a cup of milk

<u>What you will need to do</u>:

Rub the butter into the flour and add the baking soda, the cream of tartar, cinnamon, ginger and salt. Mix thoroughly.

Melt the treacle in a little of the milk and stir into the mixture. Add just enough of the remaining milk to make a firm dough.

Turn out onto a floured board and knead lightly then roll out 3mm thick and cut into triangles.

Bake in a greased tin in a hot oven (200 degrees C) for 10 to 15 minutes.

Clap scones

SERVES 6

What you will need:

1 cup of flour

A half teaspoon of salt

Boiling water

Honey

What you will need to do:

Sieve the flour into a bowl and add the salt. Pour over as much boiling water as necessary to make a pliable dough.

Roll into very thin rounds (as thin as you can make them) and pat with flour if required.

Bake on a hot girdle or non-stick frying pan.

It is important that, when nearly cool, you pile them one on top of the other and roll them. They should not be kept flat. Store temporarily in a tea towel.

Serve with honey.

Drop scones (also known as Scotch pancakes)

WHAT YOU WILL NEED:

1 cup of plain flour

Half a teaspoon of baking soda

1 teaspoon of cream of tartar

1 tablespoon of caster sugar

2 eggs

Half a cup of milk

What you will need to do:

Sift the flour, sugar, baking soda and cream of tartar into a bowl. Beat the eggs and add them with the milk to the bowl. Mix to a batter

Spoon the mixture onto a hot, greased griddle (or thick frying pan)

The scones will rise and bubble. Turn when golden on the one side and gently brown on the other.

SWEET PUDDINGS AND PIES

Eve's Pudding

SERVES 6-8

What you will need:

8 large cooking apples

400g of self-raising flour

400g of brown sugar

1 cup of raisins

300g of unsalted butter

6 eggs

What you will need to do:

Peel, core and slice the apples.

Grease a large serving dish with some of the butter

Place the sliced apples in the dish and scatter the raisins on top.

Beat the remaining butter and sugar together until it is creamed then beat in the eggs. Carefully fold in the flour then spread the batter over the apples

Bake for approximately 45 minutes

Queen of Puddings

SERVES 6

What you will need:

Three quarters of a pint of milk

50g of butter

The rind of a lemon

1 tablespoon of caster sugar

1 cup of fresh white breadcrumbs

2 eggs

1 tablespoon of jam

What you will need to do:

Bring the milk nearly to the boil then add the butter, the lemon rind and the half of the sugar

Separate the eggs

Put the breadcrumbs in a bowl and pour over the hot mixture and stir in the egg yolks

Leave to stand for 10 minutes then pour it into a lightly greased pie dish (2-pint dish)

Bake in a moderate oven (180 degrees C) for approximately 20 minutes (until set)

Cover the pudding with the jam

Whisk the egg whites and pour over the pudding

Sprinkle the remaining sugar on top

Reduce the oven to 150 degrees C and return the pudding

Bake for a further 15 minutes (until the top is a toasted a light gold.

Almond Florry

SERVES 6

What you will need:

450g of finely crushed almonds

900g of rough puff pastry

Quarter of a cup of orange flower water

8 eggs

Half a cup of cream

Half a glass of brandy

200g of clarified butter

450g of currants

2 tablespoons of sugar

A teaspoon of ground cinnamon

A half a teaspoon of nutmeg

What you will need to do:

Blanch the almonds in the orange flower water.

Separate the eggs and discard 4 of the egg whites. Beat the remaining 4 yolks with the other 4 eggs and mix in the cream, the brandy, the butter, currants, sugar, cinnamon and nutmeg.

Line a dish with half of the rough puff pastry and pour in the mixture. Cover with the remaining pastry and bake in a hot oven for 45 minutes or until the pastry is cooked.

Apple Florry

SERVES 6

What you will need:

8 apples

900g of rough puff pastry

2 tablespoons of sugar

2 tablespoons of orange marmalade

A cup of water

A teaspoon of ground cinnamon

The rind of one lemon

What you will need to do:

Melt the sugar in the water. Add the cinnamon and

Peel, core and slice the apples and add to the sugar water. Simmer for 5 minutes then add the lemon rind.

Line a dinner plate with half of the pastry and cover with the apples. Spread over the marmalade and cover with the remaining pastry.

Bake in a hot oven for 45 minutes or until the pastry is cooked.

Prune Florry

MAKE AS APPLE FLORRY but replace the apples with 500g of stoned prunes and add a squeeze of lemon and a tablespoon of port.

Apple Pudding

SERVES 4

What you will need:

6 apples

900g of rough puff pastry

170g of butter

4 eggs

A tablespoon of orange flower water

A tablespoon of brandy

1 teaspoon of sugar

The rind of one lemon

2 leftover plain biscuits

What you will need to do:

Peel, core and grate the apples and add the butter and beat until it resembles thick cream.

Beat the eggs and add to the mixture. Mix in the orange water, the brandy and the sugar.

Grind the biscuits and add to the mix with the sugar. Mix thoroughly.

Line a pie dish with pastry and add the mix. Cover with the remaining pastry and bake in a hot oven for 45 minutes or until the pastry is cooked.

Biscuit Pudding

SERVES 4-6

What you will need:

6 leftover biscuits

2 cups of milk

4 eggs

1 cup of sugar

1 tablespoon of butter

1 teaspoon of vanilla extract

What you will need to do:

Break up the biscuits and soak in a cup of milk and stand for 10 minutes then beat in one of the eggs and the sugar. Beat in the remaining eggs one at a time.

Melt the butter and add to the mixture. Then add the remaining cup of milk and he vanilla extract.

Pour into a buttered pudding dish and put in a preheated moderate oven for 50 minutes or until a knife pushed into the middle comes out clean and dry.

Drumlanrig Pudding

SERVES 4-6

<u>What you will need</u>:

6 stalks of rhubarb

Half a loaf of bread

Sugar to taste

<u>What you will need to do</u>:

Stew the rhubarb in sugared water. Layer the bread into a greased pudding basin and add the rhubarb. Add another layer of bread and then more rhubarb. Continue layering until the dish is full. Cover with a large plate and leave for 24 hours in the fridge.

(You can make this dish with raspberries, strawberries and currants instead of the rhubarb|.)

Apple Puddings in Skins

SERVES 6

What you will need:

6 apples

4 leftover biscuits

1 cup of minced suet

1 tablespoon of sugar

1 glass of white wine

A teaspoon of ground cinnamon

Half a teaspoon of nutmeg

1 tablespoon of butter

What you will need to do:

Do not peel the apples but use a corer to remove each of the cores.

Pound the biscuits and add the suet, the sugar. The cinnamon and the nutmeg and mix in the wine. Spoon the mixture into the apples but not too full as it will swell.

Place side by side on a greased baking tray and share the tablespoon of butter by placing a small knop on the top of each apple.

Put in a moderate oven for 20 minutes or until the apples are cooked through.

Clootie Dumpling (version 1)

SERVES 12

<u>What you will need</u>:

450g of flour

Half a cup of shredded suet

Half a cup of fresh breadcrumbs

Half a cup of sugar

1 teaspoon of mixed spice

Half a teaspoon of salt

A grated apple

1 cup of sultanas

One and a half cups of raisins

1 tablespoon of golden syrup

250mls of milk

<u>What you will need to do</u>:

Mix all of the ingredients thoroughly.

Scald a cloth in boiling water and dust with flour

Place the mixture on the cloth and tie securely but ensure that you leave plenty of room for the mixture to swell.

Place a plate on the bottom of a large pan of boiling water and place the pudding on top of the plate.

Cover and boil for 3 to 4 hours, topping up with boiling water throughout.

When cooked, remove the cloth gently and dry out the pudding for a few minutes in the oven.

Clootie Dumpling (version 2)

SERVES 12

<u>What you will need</u>:

450g of flour

Half a cup of shredded suet

Half a cup of brown sugar

1 teaspoon of mixed spice

1 teaspoon of cinnamon

Half a teaspoon of salt

A grated apple

450g of mixed fruit (sultanas, raisins, currants)

Half a teaspoon of bicarbonate of soda

2 tablespoons of treacle

250mls of full fat milk

<u>What you will need to do</u>:

In an extra-large bowl, mix the flour, fruit, sugar, spice, cinnamon, suet and bicarbonate of soda

Add the salt, the treacle and some of the milk (enough to make the mixture slightly sloppy)

Scald a cloth in boiling water and dust finely with flour

Put the mixture on the cloth and secure with string (leaving enough room to allow the mixture to swell)

Place a plate in the bottom of a large pan of boiling water and place the pudding on top of the plate

Half fill the pan with boiling water.

Cover and boil for 3 to 4 hours, topping up the water throughout.

When cooked, remove gently from the cloth and dry out the pudding for a few minutes in a pre-heated oven.

Currant Duff

SERVES 6

What you will need:

400g of flour

1 cup of shredded suet

1 cup of currants

Half a cup of caster sugar

Finely grated rind of 1 orange

Water

What you will need to do:

Sift the flour into a bowl and stir in the suet, currants, rind and sugar.

Stir in enough water to make a medium consistency batter. Butter a pudding basin and add the mixture and steam for two and a half hours then turn onto a warm plate.

Apple Meringue Pie

WHAT YOU WILL NEED:

For the flan case: 250g of plain flour

125g butter

2 tablespoons caster sugar

1 egg yolk

1 tablespoon cold water

For the apple meringue:

6 apples

100g brown sugar

125g white sugar

2 tablespoons of jam (preferably plum)

2 tablespoons of flour

2 tablespoons of cream

1 egg yolk and 2 egg whites

What you will need to do:

For the flan: brush a flan tin with melted butter ((9-inch flan tin)

Sift the flour and rub in the butter until it resembles fine breadcrumbs then add the sugar. Add the egg yolk and the water and mix to form soft dough.

Wrap in cling-film and rest in the fridge for 20 minutes then roll out, line the flan tin and prick all over with a fork.

Blind bake (cover with greaseproof paper and weigh down with the weights of choice (baking beads, dried beans, dried rice etc.). Bake for 30 minutes at 180 degrees C.

For the apple meringue:

Peel, core and thinly slice the apples and place in the flan case.

Beat the egg yolk with the cream and then mix in the brown sugar and the flour. Pour and spread the mixture over the apples.

Bake in a hot oven (220 degrees C) for 10 minutes, reduce the heat to 180 degrees C and bake for a further 20 minutes

Make the meringue by whisking the egg whites and gradually adding the sugar. Spread the jam over the apple and top the pie with the meringue.

Bake in the oven (180 degrees C) for twenty minutes

Drunken Rhubarb and Whisky Pie

WHAT YOU WILL NEED:

Make the flan case (see the flan recipe for apple meringue pie)

500g of rhubarb

75mls of whisky

1 tablespoon of caster sugar

1 egg yolk

Half a teaspoon of ground ginger

What you will need to do:

Bake the flan as per the recipe only use a 7-inch flan tin (and keep the spare pastry to one side)

Cut the rhubarb into small chunks and place in the flan case. Sprinkle over the whisky, the sugar and the ground ginger

Use the remaining pastry to place narrow strips across the rhubarb (twists of pastry look nice)

Put the pie back in the oven and bake for 20 minutes or until the rhubarb has softened.

CAKES AND SWEET LOAVES

MY WEE GRANNY'S FULL TABLE

Fruit Cake (version 1)

SERVES 6

<u>What you will need</u>:

340g of plain flour

170g brown sugar

170g sultanas

170g currants

170g raisins

50g chopped cherries

280ml milk

30g candied peel

Half a teaspoon mixed spice

Half teaspoon cinnamon

Quarter of a teaspoon nutmeg

70g butter

Teaspoon bicarbonate of soda

<u>What you will need to do</u>:

Sift the flour and mix in the spices

Rub in the butter and sugar and then add the fruit and the peel

Gently heat the milk to take the chill off and mix in the bicarbonate of soda then mix thoroughly through the cake mix

Grease a 17cm square baking tin,

Add the mixture

Bake at 180 degrees C for one hour, reduce the heat and bake for a further hour at 160 degrees C

Fruit Cake (version 2 – with whisky)

SERVES 6

<u>What you will need</u>:

400mls of malt whisky

30g of ground almonds

200g of self-raising flour

170g brown sugar

600g of mixed fruit (sultanas, currants, raisins)

100g of mixed peel

3 eggs

A teaspoon mixed spice

Half teaspoon cinnamon

Quarter of a teaspoon nutmeg

150g butter

Teaspoon bicarbonate of soda

<u>What you will need to do</u>:

Soak the fruit in the whisky for at least 12 hours (longer if possible). If left in the fridge, remember to bring back to room temperature before adding to the mix

Cream the butter and sugar

Whisk the eggs and gently stir into the creamed mixture

Add the fruit and the whisky

Sift the flour and mix in the spices and the almonds then add to the mixture and mix thoroughly

Rub in the butter and sugar and then add the fruit and the peel

Grease and line a square baking tin, add the mixture and bake in a pre-heated oven (180 degrees C) for one hour and then cover the top with foil and bake for a further 45 minutes

Black Bun

(THIS IS AN EXTREMELY rich fruit cake that will help to soak up the alcohol consumed on Hogmanay)

What you will need:

For the pastry case: (the cake is baked in a loaf tin that has been lined with the pastry)

340g of plain flour

170g of butter

Pinch of salt

Half a teaspoon of baking powder

Half a cup of Cold water

For the cake:

170g of plain flour

500g of raisins

500g of currants

Teaspoon of allspice

Teaspoon of ground ginger

Teaspoon of cinnamon

Teaspoon of baking powder

One tablespoon brandy

One large, beaten egg

2 tablespoons of milk

WHAT YOU WILL NEED to do:

For the pastry:

Sift the flour and rub in the butter then add the salt. Add enough of the water to form a firm dough (it has to be firm to line the loaf tin and hold the cake)

Roll out the pastry

You need to place the pastry in the loaf tin in pieces, so roughly measure the bottom, the 4 sides and the top cut it into 6 appropriate lengths

Place the bottom and 4 sides in the tin – ensuring the sides overlap. Keep the remaining (top) until you add the cake mixture

For the cake:

Sift the flour and add the sugar, all of the fruit, the peel, the spices and the almonds and mix thoroughly then bind the mixture together by adding the brandy and half of the beaten egg. Add some milk to further moisten.

Once it is thoroughly mixed, put into the pastry case and add the pastry lid. Use the remaining egg to seal the edges and to create a glaze.

Prick the surface all over with a fork and use a skewer to place 4 holes from the lid to the base.

Bake for approximately three hours in a low to moderate oven (160 degrees C)

Montrose Cakes

WHAT YOU WILL NEED:

100g of self-raising flower

100g of caster sugar

100g of butter

75g of currants

1 tablespoon brandy

quarter of a teaspoon of ground nutmeg

2 eggs

2 teaspoons of rose water

What you will need to do:

Beat the eggs. Cream the butter and sugar then add the eggs. Mix thoroughly then add the currants, the brandy, the rose water and nutmeg. Stir in the flour.

When thoroughly mixed, share and spoon the mixture into 24 paper cases (cupcake cases) which have been placed in cupcake tin and bake in a hot oven (190 degrees C) for 10 to 15 minutes

Marmalade Cake

WHAT YOU WILL NEED:

226g of self-raising flour

2 eggs

2 tablespoons of milk

75g of caster sugar

100g of butter

2 tablespoons of marmalade (preferably orange)

1 teaspoon of finely grated orange rind

What you will need to do:

Sift the flour and rub in the butter until the mixture resembles fine breadcrumbs then add the sugar and the orange rind. Beat the eggs and add to the mix then add the marmalade and the milk

Mix thoroughly

Grease a 6-inch cake tin and add the mixture

Bake in a moderate oven (170 degrees C) for approximately 80 minutes

Dundee Cake

WHAT YOU WILL NEED:

226g of plain flour

75g of butter

140g of caster sugar

Tablespoon of finely chopped almonds

12 blanched whole almonds (split in 2)

4 eggs

Teaspoon of baking powder

500g of mixed fruit (sultanas, raisins, currants)

Tablespoon of mixed peel

2 tablespoons of whisky

For the glaze – 2 tablespoons of warm milk sweetened with a teaspoon of sugar

What you will need to do:

Cream the butter and sugar and slowly add the eggs and most of the flour (a spoonful at a time) then add the chopped almonds and the fruit and the remaining flour Mix through the whisky and ensure everything is mixed thoroughly.

Put the mixture in a greased and lined 8-inch cake tin and cover with greaseproof paper. Bake in a moderate oven (170 degrees C) and after one hour, remove the paper and add the milk glaze then place the split almonds on top and bake for a further hour.

Gingerbread Loaf

WHAT YOU WILL NEED:

22g of butter

200g of brown sugar

200g of treacle

500g of self-raising flour

2 teaspoons of powdered ginger

1 teaspoon of baking soda

200mls of milk

What you will need to do:

Cream the butter, sugar and treacle

Sieve the flour and the ginger and add to the treacle mix. Add the baking soda and some of the milk (enough to make a soft consistency)

Grease a 2lb loaf tin

Bake in a moderate oven (170 degrees C) for 90 minutes

Sultana Loaf (version 1)

SERVES 6

<u>What you will need</u>:

500g of plain flour

1 teaspoon bicarbonate of soda

200g of butter

200g of brown sugar

200g of sultanas

3 eggs

300ml milk

<u>What you will need to do</u>:

Sift the flour and mix in the bicarbonate of soda then rub the butter into the flour until it resembles breadcrumbs

Add the sugar and the sultanas and then mix through the milk. Add the beaten eggs

Turn out into a greased 2lb loaf tin

Bake in a moderate oven (180 degrees C) for 90 minutes or until fully cooked through

Sultana Loaf (version 2)

SERVES 6

<u>What you will need</u>:

250g of plain flour

250g of wholemeal flour

2 teaspoons of mixed spice

1 teaspoon bicarbonate of soda

170g of butter

200g of brown sugar

200g of sultanas

1 egg

300ml milk

<u>What you will need to do</u>:

Sift the plain and wholemeal flour with the spice and mix in the bicarbonate of soda then rub the butter into the flour until it resembles breadcrumbs

Add the sugar and the sultanas and then mix through the milk. Add the beaten egg

Turn out into a greased 2lb loaf tin

Bake in a moderate oven (180 degrees C) for 90 minutes or until fully cooked through

Bran Loaf

SERVES 6

<u>What you will need</u>:

112g of All Bran cereal

280g of mixed fruit (sultanas, currants, raisons)

280ml of milk

140g of caster sugar

112g of self-raising flour

<u>What you will need to do</u>:

Mix the bran, fruit and sugar in a bowl

Add the milk and allow to stand and soak through for 30 minutes

Mix in the flour

Grease and line a 2lb loaf tin and add the mixture

Bake in a moderate to high oven (180 degrees C) for 60 minutes

Cool in the tin

Currant Duff

SERVES 6

What you will need:

400g of flour

1 cup of shredded suet

1 cup of currants

Half a cup of caster sugar

Finely grated rind of 1 orange

Water

What you will need to do:

Sift the flour into a bowl and stir in the suet, currants, rind and sugar.

Stir in enough water to make a medium consistency batter. Butter a pudding basin and add the mixture and steam for two and a half hours then turn onto a warm plate.

Boiled Fruit Loaf (version 1)

SERVES 6-8

<u>What you will need</u>:

230g of self-raising flour

112g of butter

112g of sugar

340g of mixed fruit (sultanas, currants and raisons)

1 egg

140mls water

<u>What you will need to do</u>:

Put the butter, fruit, sugar and water into a saucepan and mix thoroughly

Bring to a gentle boil and simmer for 20 minutes

Cool and then beat the egg and add to the mix

Mix in the flour and when thoroughly mixed, pour into a lined and greased 2lb loaf tin

Bake in a moderate oven (160 degrees) for 90 minutes

Boiled Fruit Loaf (version 2)

SERVES 8-10

<u>What you will need</u>:

450g of self-raising flour

2 cups of sultanas

225g of butter

2 cups of milk

2 eggs

1 teaspoon of bicarbonate of soda

<u>What you will need to do</u>:

Mix the sultanas, milk, sugar and butter together in a saucepan and bring to a gentle boil

Simmer for 5 minutes

Cool and then mix in the flour and bicarbonate of soda. Beat the eggs and add to the mix

Share the mixture between 2 x 1lb loaf tins

Bake in a moderate oven (160 degrees) for 45 minutes to 60 minutes

Date and Walnut Loaf

SERVES 10-12

What you will need:

12 oz. self-raising flour

8oz butter

8oz dark brown sugar

8oz walnuts

340g dates (ensure thoroughly de-stoned)

1 teaspoon bicarbonate of soda

Half a pint of water

2 eggs

What you will need to do:

Put the butter, sugar and dates into a saucepan and add the water then bring to a gentle boil. Simmer for 5 minutes

Cool and mash and then add the bicarbonate of soda. Chop the walnuts and add to the mix

Beat the eggs and add to the mixture then add the

the flour

Grease 3 x 1lb loaf tins and share the mix between the tins

Bake in moderate oven (160 degrees C) for 60-90 minutes

Raisin Tray-Bake

SERVES 12

What you will need:

450g plain flour

225g butter

Water

450g raisins

1 teaspoon mixed spice

Half teaspoon cinnamon

Dessert spoon cornflour

1 tablespoon of sugar

Icing sugar

1 cup of desiccated coconut

What you will need to do:

Make the pastry by mixing the flour and butter to a fine breadcrumb consistency and add enough cold water to bind. Wrap in cling-film and chill for at least 30 minutes in the fridge

Put the raisins in a large saucepan and add sugar, mixed spice and cinnamon

Cover with water, bring to a gentle boil and simmer for 5 minutes

Mix cornflour with a little water and add to the mix to thicken

Allow to cool

Roll out pastry

Grease a large baking tray and line with the pastry

Add the cooled fruit

Bake in a moderate oven (180 degrees) for approximately 30 minutes.

Make up (thin) glace icing using the icing sugar and water

When the bake is completely cool cover with the icing and sprinkle on the desiccated coconut.

BISCUITS AND SHORTBREAD

Shortbread (version 1)

YOU WILL NEED:

240g of plain flour

120g of cornflour

120g of icing sugar.

225g of butter

Caster sugar for sprinkling on top

What you will need to do:

Cream the butter and the icing sugar until it is smooth and creamy. Sieve the flour and mix in until it forms a dough.

Rest the dough wrapped in cling film in the fridge for 20 minutes.

To roll – place between two sheets of cling film and roll out quite thick (half an inch at least).

Cut into fingers or rounds (for petticoat tails, put in a round baking tin and mark out lightly with a knife)

Prick the surface with a fork and bake in a medium oven (160 degrees C) for about 20 minutes or until they are a pale golden colour.

Sprinkle with sugar and cool on a wire tray.

Shortbread (version 2 – chocolate chip)

WHAT YOU WILL NEED:

200g of plain flour

25g of cocoa

200g of butter

100g of chocolate chips

85g of caster sugar

What you will need to do:

Make as version one, but sift the cocoa with the flour and add the chocolate chips to the mix at the dough stage.

Shortbread (version 3 – stem ginger)

WHAT YOU WILL NEED:

200g of plain flour

100g of caster sugar

200g of butter

100g of semolina

2 teaspoons of ground ginger

8 pieces of stem ginger

Teaspoon of brown sugar

What you will need to do:

Make as version one, but sift the semolina and the ground ginger with the flour then chop the stem ginger and add to the mix at the dough stage.

Shortbread (version 4 – caramel)

WHAT YOU WILL NEED:

For the shortbread base:

200g of plain flour

150g of butter

75g of caster sugar

For the filling:

25g of butter

25g of brown sugar

A tin (397g) of condensed milk

For the topping:

200g of milk chocolate

What you will need to do:

For the shortbread base:

Sieve the flour and rub in the butter until the mixture resembles fine breadcrumbs. Mix in the sugar. Line a 9-inch square sandwich tin with greaseproof paper then pour in and firm down the mixture. Bake in a moderate oven (170 degrees C) for approximately 30 minutes or until golden brown.

Allow to cool

For the filling:

Add the condensed milk, the butter and the sugar to a pan and gently heat – stirring continuously – until the mixture thickens then spread the mixture over the (cooled) shortbread base and allow to cool

For the topping:

Melt the chocolate and spread over the (cooled) filling and allow to set

Cut into squares

Empire Biscuits

FOR EMPIRE BISCUITS use the recipe for shortbread (version 1) but roll out thinner and cut into rounds. Bake for less time and remove just as the biscuits are changing colour (keep a close eye on them and remove from the oven as SOON as they change colour. These biscuits burn very quickly. They may appear soft, but the will crisp up as they cool)

When cool (cool on a wire tray) sandwich with raspberry jam and cover with icing (glace – icing sugar and water).

Oaties (version 1)

WHAT YOU WILL NEED:

112g of plain flour

2 teaspoons of baking powder

Half teaspoon of salt

112g of rolled oats

50g of caster sugar

75g of treacle

112g of butter

What you will need to do:

Sieve the flour, baking powder and salt and add the rolled oats. Heat the sugar, treacle and butter in a pan until melted then mix it into the flour. Mix thoroughly and then press into a 7-inch greased sandwich tin and bake in a moderate oven (170 degrees C) for 20 minutes.

Cut into wedges and cool on a wire tray.

Oaties (version 2)

WHAT YOU WILL NEED:

30mls of melted bacon fat

A quarter of a teaspoon of bicarbonate of soda

A quarter of a teaspoon of salt

200g of rolled oats

Two tablespoons of warm water

What you will need to do:

Mix the majority of the oats, the bicarbonate of soda and the salt together with the melted bacon fat and mix to a dough with the water.

Put the remaining oats on a board and turn out the dough onto the board, knead and then roll out into a thin round

Cut into 3 triangles (farls) and cook on an ungreased girdle (or heavy frying pan) until crisp (not brown) turn and cook for a minute on the other side.

Tantallon Biscuits

WHAT YOU WILL NEED:

112g of plain flour

112g of rice flour

A pinch of baking soda

112g of butter

112g of sugar

2 eggs

3 drops of lemon essence

What you will need to do:

Beat the eggs. Sieve the plain flour, the rice flour and the baking soda. Cream the butter and the sugar and then mix a little of the egg with a spoonful of the flour mix and continue until all ingredients are thoroughly combined then add the lemon essence and stir in.

Roll out thinly and cut into rounds

Bake on a greased baking sheet in a moderate to hot oven (180 degrees C) for 30 minutes

Cool on a wire tray

Abernethy Biscuits

WHAT YOU WILL NEED:

225g of plain flour

Half a teaspoon of baking powder

100g of butter

100g of caster sugar

1 teaspoon of caraway seeds

1 egg

A tablespoon of milk

What you will need to do:

Sieve the flour and the baking powder and rub in the butter and then add the sugar and the caraway seeds. Beat the egg and add to the mix and add the milk to form a stiff dough. Roll out thinly on a floured board and cut into rounds.

Bake on a greased baking sheet in a moderate oven (160 degrees C) for 10 minutes

Ginger Biscuits

WHAT YOU WILL NEED:

112g of self-raising flour

2 teaspoons of ground ginger

10g of caster sugar

Half a teaspoon of bicarbonate of soda

112g of butter

112g of golden syrup

A tablespoon of milk

What you will need to do:

Sieve the flour, sugar, bicarbonate of soda and the ginger.

Add the syrup and the butter to a pan and melt without boiling. Cool and add the mix.

Roll mixture into small balls and place on a greased baking sheet. Allow plenty of space between as the balls will spread.

Dip a pastry brush in the milk and use it to slightly flatten the balls.

Bake in a low to moderate oven (160 degrees C) for 10 minutes. They should be firm but not hard.

Cool on a wire tray

Walnut Biscuits:

WHAT YOU WILL NEED:

200g of plain flour

150g of caster sugar

1 teaspoon of baking powder

112g of butter

50g of finely chopped walnuts

1 egg

What you will need to do:

Beat the egg. Sieve the flour and the baking powder and rub in the butter until it resembles fine breadcrumbs. Add the caster sugar and the walnuts and add the egg.

Turn out onto a floured board and knead thoroughly before rolling out thinly and cutting into rounds

Bake on a greased baking sheet in a moderate to hot oven (190 degrees C) until golden brown (should only take 5 or 10 minutes)

Cool on a wire tray

Thank you for reading my wee granny's recipes. I hope you get many years of enjoyment in cooking, baking and eating.

Printed in Great Britain
by Amazon